I0816264

worry medicine

REMEDIES AND RITUALS FOR ANXIOUS TIMES

NINA MONTENEGRO

For the little ones—
Lucia, Rio, Sula, and Iris.

contents

healing is always available to us—

as the zen teaching goes,

the whole world is our medicine.

it is in spite of sorrow that we find joy.

it is **because** *of sorrow that we find joy.*

introduction

Trucks barrel along the road behind me as I part the dense burdock and cleavers that form the protective edge of the forest. Burrs grab hold of my jacket, needling me to slow down and move more mindfully as I pick my way through the thicket. Finally, I've gained passage—the understory opens up, revealing towering hardwoods, their leaves an illuminated mosaic overhead. Leaving the low rumble of traffic behind, I call to mind the question I came here to ask, speaking it aloud so that all who are listening will hear: "What do I need in order to heal?" I have come hoping I will receive some nudge toward a remedy for my mysterious physical symptoms—most urgently, the eczema erupting on my elbows and neck. But I sense that I am also in search of a deeper healing: medicine to soothe an unsettled soul.

I walk a little farther, placing my hand on the furrowed bark of a tree, letting it linger there. I begin to notice that the trunk of this tree, and all the trees around it, has pocks and blackened dark spots, as imperfect as my own skin. Some trunks have holes; some have scars where old wounds have healed over. One tree's bark has swallowed a piece of barbed-wire fencing. Not a tree in this forest is blemish-free, reminding me that we don't go through this life unscathed—emotionally or physically. We are decorated by our stories. And despite the pocks, the wounds, and the scars, I notice how incredibly alive and thriving these tree beings are. Their bodies are resilient, healing with the support of the medicine around them: the breeze in which they sway, the frogs whose song vibrates their leaves, the soft rain nourishing their roots, the neighboring trees that offer company. Perhaps even my presence—my loving gaze and gentle touch—is medicine for them.

The response I hear is this: The medicine is already here. It's within us and all around us. True healing is possible when we expand our understanding of medicine to include not only what we consume (read: buy) but what we experience, embody, and do. In the simplest sense, medicine is in how we choose to live our lives. It's in how we engage with the world.

"Worry medicine" takes countless forms: a mantra on repeat, a song we love, a nourishing walk, a prayer. This book invites us to dive deep into the diversity and abundance of medicine within reach. Like a tree laden with ripe fruit, it bears delicious folk wisdom for healing, wherein "folk" means, simply, "by and for the people." Story by story, we will explore generations-old strategies for navigating the worry that comes with being alive.

So often, worry is spoken about and treated in medical terms. Chronic worry becomes "anxiety," and patterns of anxiety are diagnosed as disorders—something wrong with an individual. While anxiety disorders are very real and serious, some level of worry is a natural response to the pressures of modern life. Not only do we need to pay the bills, care for others, and manage our health but we must also cope with innumerable systemic stressors: legacies of capitalism, colonialism, racism, and patriarchy drive increased disconnection and isolation, ecological destruction, and the erosion of our rights and democracy, not to mention modern crises of meaning. These undercurrents have a very real effect on our mental and physical health. As sensitive beings hardwired to keep ourselves and those we love safe, how could we not be anxious? And because it seems nearly impossible to lead a completely worry-free life, why aren't we taught from an early age how to live with worry?

This book is not meant to prescribe; rather, it is intended to invite experimentation, to illuminate possible paths. I am not a therapist or a doctor but an artist. As such, my suggestions aren't limited to one modality—they go wide and deep, rooting around for both personal and universal truths.

For fifteen years, I've kept a "worry journal" filled with practices I turn to in periods of disquiet. In that time, I've noticed a marked increase in anxiety among many people. I myself have experienced more anxiety in the last decade or so, and I've watched as friends and acquaintances have struggled to cope. So I decided to make my worry journal available as a zine. This book is an expansion and outgrowth of that zine. It draws from an array of personal experiences, modalities, and traditions to offer a first aid kit for anxious times—but one that is meant to be used flexibly. Fashion your own kit by taking whatever serves you and leaving the rest. Build on what you find here, deepen it, and make it yours. Read the pages in sequence or pick one at random to find the medicine that calls to you.

Writing and illustrating this book has been healing for me, and I hope that, in some small way, reading it helps you heal too.

my

joy

is bigger than my fear

a pomegranate in winter

In early winter, when pomegranate season begins, I drop everything and make my way to the supermarket to meet the ruby fruits that have arrived from far away. When I bring one home, my two small daughters clamor to crack it open. They do, sweet red juice spraying every which way, messily dripping down cheeks and hands. The three of us share the same fruit, relishing its sweet abundance. A pomegranate is so easily shared, a jewel to each of eight hundred tongues—a burst of juicy decadence for all.

Even in seasons of scarcity, there is joy to find and savor. A boisterous laugh overheard on the bus, steam curling in buttery sunlight, the embrace of a cozy wool sweater, a new favorite song. A powerful counterweight to worry, joy is primarily found in the present; it requires that we inhabit our bodies, tuning our senses to the physical world around us. Lately, when a worry springs up, I've been whispering to myself: "My joy is bigger than my fear." Yet a capacity for joy takes practice—if we let our worries take over, our vision clouds, and we neglect to see the gifts before us. By contrast, consciously noticing and attending to what moves and delights us will reduce worry and build lasting contentment.

We tend to feel guilty for experiencing joy while others are suffering. We may even be ashamed to glimpse joy in the midst of our own grief. But this is precisely when joy is needed most. The Ukrainian-born poet Ilya Kaminsky put this beautifully: "Is it foolish to speak of little joys that occur in the middle of tragedy? It is our humanity. Whatever we have left of it. We must not deny it to ourselves."

Consciously or unconsciously, many of us keep a running list of grievances. What if we listed our joys instead? Start by keeping a weekly log of what brings you amusement or pleasure, and if that goes well, move to a daily list. Sometimes, this alone is enough to increase gratitude overall and dissolve worry, but challenge yourself to take the celebration further. Choose a handful of joys to expound upon. In art, writing, song, or whatever comes naturally, express what it is about those joys you find so special.

Make an altar to that which brings you joy. Gather a branch or stone from a special place, a picture of someone who has inspired you, an object you treasured as a child, a piece of ripe fruit. In an intentional way, arrange these things on a dresser, shelf, mantel, or other surface you dedicate to this purpose. Tend to the altar in the coming days by visiting it regularly. Add or subtract objects, rearrange them, and periodically clean the altar. Touch or hold the objects, expressing your gratitude for each of them and what they represent, or simply sit before them, letting your soft gaze be a meditation.

the uninvited guest

Wild morning glory, also called bindweed, is a tenacious plant. Once it has found its way into a garden, it can quickly take over, suffocating other plants and occupying space intended for fruit, vegetables, or flowers. When I lived on an organic farm, this vigorous plant had taken hold in a crucial growing area. We tried starving it of sunlight by laying down black tarps. Frustratingly (yet admirably), the bindweed always found its way to the light, trailing underneath the tarps, then climbing everything in sight. We tried to dig it up, but its runners and roots would inevitably snap off in the soil—leaving little bits behind to proliferate. The more forcefully we cut it back, the more intensely it would surge forth. Finally, we learned that morning glory thrives in poor, dry soils. If we could improve the soil and increase its moisture content, the plant might leave of its own accord. We set about a multiyear project of enriching the soil, thickly layering it with compost and manure every chance we got—and it worked. The morning glory receded.

Worry itself can act like a perennial weed, an uninvited guest. Like the morning glory, worry threatens to overtake and constrain us. In fact, the word "worry" comes from the Old English *wyrgan*, meaning "to strangle." We feel cornered and immobilized by our worries. At the same time, when we worry, we are also doing the strangling, attempting to wrench into our control what is likely beyond it. It's tempting to believe that our worrying is productive, that, somehow, by ruminating on an issue, we can change it. In reality, this is almost never true—we are only moving in circles, binding ourselves more tightly with each loop.

When you find yourself worrying, check in with your body and ask yourself a few questions: Am I hungry? Could I use a walk? Would a fifteen-minute nap serve me? Does gathering with friends sound appealing, or does a stretch of solitude? When we nourish ourselves in body and spirit, we create an environment in which worry is unwelcome, from which it naturally recedes.

At the end of a long day, if I'm beginning to feel overwhelmed, I often remember an old saying my grandfather used to repeat: "We're optimists in the morning, realists in the afternoon, and pessimists at night." Notice the conditions in which your worries flourish. If you worry most in the evenings, acknowledge this and plan for it. Remind yourself that your resources are depleted at night, but they'll replenish by morning. Rather than spin your wheels, commit to setting your troubles aside until you're better equipped to deal with them. (You may notice they appear less worrisome after a good night's sleep.)

Sometimes, our attempts to relieve our worries can actually cause them to proliferate. For example, if you have anxiety about your health, are you regularly researching your symptoms? Do you observe a spike in anxiety when you do? Identify what triggers or inflames your worry and begin to set boundaries for yourself. To help shift your behavior, commit to replacing unhelpful habits with healthful ones. For example, when you have the urge to research your symptoms, commit to taking five deep breaths or drinking a full glass of water instead.

CALMNESS

IN CHAOS

the quiet place below

Growing up on the shores of Lake Michigan, I learned that, on a very wavy day, the best way to swim out is to dive under the waves rather than fight them at the surface, which quickly drains our energy. Beneath the tumultuous surface, the waters are calmer, allowing for easier progress.

When life feels particularly challenging, we can dive beneath the chaotic waters of the outer world to access a deep reserve of inner calm. This interior refuge is always available to us, even in times of storm. This is the quiet place below, the place of equanimity, the root of our resilience. Instead of exhausting ourselves by thrashing about and trying to stay afloat, we can learn to return to our quiet place again and again. Each time we visit, it becomes easier to reside there.

Practice finding a place of inner calm amidst outer chaos. In a loud train station, airport, market, or even in your own bustling home, experiment with sitting down and closing your eyes for one to three minutes. Notice how your perception shifts when you turn off visual input. Let the surrounding sounds rise and fall without attaching to or judging them. Each time you feel distracted, gently return your focus to your breath. Eventually, with enough practice, you may find you're able to access "the quiet place below" without even closing your eyes.

On the eve of a day when you have no other commitments, cover all your clocks. Turn off your phone and store it safely out of sight. Place a strip of electrical tape over the clocks on your kitchen appliances, computer, and car dashboard. Unplug or drape cloth over any other clocks in your home. Allow yourself to orient to the natural rhythms of the day. While this may feel unnerving at first, give yourself a chance to adjust. Remember that seconds, minutes, and hours are merely constructions, and without them, our perception may change, but the physical world remains constant. The rhythms of nature will persist; the sun will rise and fall at the usual pace. At the start of your clock-free day, wake without an alarm, whenever your body is ready. Eat when you feel hungry, not when the clock says it's mealtime. Avoid dividing the day's activities into timed increments. Instead, engage in things for as long as you feel inclined. Fall into bed when you're tired and ready, and when you wake the next morning, reflect on the sense of spaciousness you experienced by living this way for a day. While clocks and schedules help us function in the modern world, an occasional day without them can greatly reduce stress and help us to realign with a pace that feels more natural.

While we may want to avoid "taking the easy way out," this is not quite the same as prioritizing ease. Sometimes, the path of least resistance is also the path to inner calm. If conversation with someone you regularly interact with feels forced, commit to engaging less with this person and more with those who allow you to be your authentic self. If you're pressed for time before dinner, order out or ask someone else to cook. If you end the week feeling drained, review your weekend plans and see what can be postponed. Perhaps you joined a book club or sports team for fun, but it's become a chore. Instead of forcing yourself to continue, give yourself permission to let it go. Fill that time with something that truly nourishes you.

what's calling to you?

the natural news

Sitting on the couch one day, scrolling through headlines on my phone, I felt an invisible nudge to get up and go outside. Immediately upon opening the front door, I was met by the roaring chatter of hundreds of starlings in the oaks above my house. A moment later, they fell silent and took flight in unison, leaving behind no more than the faint reverberation of wingbeats. A deep appreciation settled over me as I watched the last few disappear beyond the distant trees.

I believe the birds called me out of the house that day to remind me of the magic I miss when I'm inside, on the computer or phone: the few moments after a rainstorm when steam rises up from the ground, iridescent beads of dew on nasturtium leaves, flickering lightning bugs, a hummingbird moth drinking from a lilac.

Often, we trade these blissful moments for time spent in the digital world: a view into the life of someone we hardly know or a steady drip of distressing news. Our constant consumption of media keeps our brains on high alert, holding us in a perpetual state of anxiety. Discontent, fear, depression, panic, and hopelessness become frequent visitors, lingering for days at a time and affecting our moods, relationships, and outlook.

By now, most of us recognize that we need breaks from technology—space for sensory experience, for real, embodied joy. But while a news or social media fast has become a common way to reset, it's easy to fill the space those activities leave behind with other equally unhealthy distractions. What if, instead of disconnecting completely, we took the opportunity to connect more meaningfully with our immediate environment?

Seek out the "natural news" in your corner of the world. Which constellations are visible in the sky tonight? What foods are in season? What's in bloom? Are the spring peepers singing? Are the Vaux's swifts visiting on their migration path? As much as possible, discover this information through observation rather than by searching online. Even better, spend an entire day outside. Post up in a chair or on a blanket in your backyard, at a park, or in a natural area. Without your normal indoor rhythms, your perception of time might change. With nothing between you and the open sky above, you may sense your thoughts expanding. Notice how you feel in both body and mind as the day unfolds.

Find an inconvenient, out-of-reach place in your house to "dock" your phone when you're not using it, like the top of a bookcase or a shelf in the basement. Removing the phone from your immediate environment will keep you from looking at it compulsively throughout the day. Instead, you'll be free to choose when to engage and when not to.

set it down

When I was in kindergarten, a "worry lady" visited our class bearing tiny fabric dolls for each of us. We learned that, in Guatemala and some parts of Mexico, people share their nighttime worries with these *muñecas quitapenas* (worry dolls), then tuck them under their pillows before going to sleep. According to Mayan legend, the dolls absorb the sleepers' worries overnight, exchanging them for wisdom. When I brought the *muñecas* home and tried this myself, I learned a lifelong lesson: Sharing the weight of my troubles with another makes them feel lighter.

Sometimes, this can look like calling a close friend or family member and asking if they have capacity to listen. Even articulating a worry—saying it aloud—seems to weaken its power. Journaling about our worries, spilling them onto the page without judgment, can have a similar unburdening effect.

Once, during a time of overwhelming anxiety, my sister left the house and went for a walk down the street. She picked up a leaf and imagined wrapping her worry inside it, then she tucked it into a nook in a tree, asking the tree to bear her burden for a while. Imagine your worry clearly, then visualize, as vividly as you can, setting it down. Tuck it somewhere—under a tree's bark, in a crack in the pavement, in between blades of grass—and ask that it be held for you there.

Sometimes, our worries feel too raw to share with friends or family. Try confiding in an animal companion instead. Animals are incredibly emotionally perceptive and, often, their silent support is just what we need. If you have a dog or cat or another sweet animal in your life, speak your worries to them. If you don't have a pet, share your troubles with the songbirds that visit your window, the honeybee that lands on your arm, or even a photo of a beloved animal companion who has passed on.

Worry can easily consume us, quickly becoming the focus of our days. To avoid runaway worry, experiment with scheduling time to reflect just as you would any other to-do. Reserve twenty minutes at, say, 7 p.m. If you find your mind drifting toward your worries throughout the day, try to set them aside, remembering that you've scheduled time to think them through later. (Be sure your worry appointment doesn't come too close to bedtime. Give yourself at least an hour before bed in which to take a walk or a bath, listen to music, or read.)

above the storm

Imagine boarding a plane on a cloudy day. The light is low, the world muted and gray. A few raindrops stream across your round window as the plane races down the runway. Rising up through the dense cloud cover, the plane wobbles and wavers before bursting through to the clear blue sky beyond. Brilliant sunlight pours in, flooding you with feelings of warmth and comfort. All at once, you're reminded: This bright sun, this cerulean sky are always here above it all, even on the dimmest, stormiest of days down below.

When my grandfather was developing severe dementia, my mom looked to the night sky for solace. She'd step outside on winter evenings and gaze at Orion—a constellation her father had shown her many years before. Though her father was slipping away, Orion remained, shining as brightly as he had in her childhood—reminding her that he had witnessed an eternity.

Even on cloudy days, the sun's most powerful rays warm us, and on dark nights, the moon continues its steadying orbit. When earthly life feels tumultuous, we can always rest in the reliability of our age-old celestial companions.

Go outside at sunrise with a cup of tea. Take in the gifts of the morning. Listen to the birds. Relish in the comfort and consistency of the sun's return. Feel the temperature change in the air and in your body as its light caresses your face. Morning sunlight boosts serotonin and is a natural mood enhancer; it delivers essential vitamin D (which is best absorbed through the skin) and helps regulate our circadian rhythms, ensuring more restful sleep. Make a ritual of bathing in natural light for at least fifteen minutes each morning.

The moon has a profound effect on water, as evidenced by the tides, which rise and fall due to its gravitational pull. Harness this powerful energy by setting a jar of clean water outside on the night of a full moon. Speak an intention into the water or write it on a small piece of paper and place the paper under the jar. The full moon is known to be a time of clarity and creation, so your intention might be something you wish to do or invite in the coming lunar cycle. Overnight, the water will absorb the moonlight and become "charged" by its energy, amplifying your wish. In the morning, you can drink this water, add it to a bath, or use it to wash your hands and face. Try this again under a waning moon, this time with an intention centered on release. Is there a worry or a habit you wish to shed? Write it down on a piece of paper, place it under your jar, and let the moon's receding energy draw it away.

reorient

Worrying produces stagnant energy and a sensation of "stuckness." A change in our environment, physical position, or even our wardrobe can prompt a shift in energy, freeing us from the ruminative cycle.

The clothing we wear has the power to transform our mood and self-image. Years ago, on a camping trip, my friend and I hadn't brought enough warm clothes, so we went to a thrift shop in a nearby town and bought wool sweaters. From then on, we called these our "adventure sweaters" and reserved them for travel. To this day, when I put on that sweater, I feel poised for spontaneity. Similarly, a graphic designer I recently met told me he changes his shoes at certain points in the day to invite different energy. He keeps a pair of sneakers in his office to change into when he transitions from morning meetings to a block of creative time in the afternoon. When he puts on the sneakers, he says he becomes a new person—more imaginative and more relaxed.

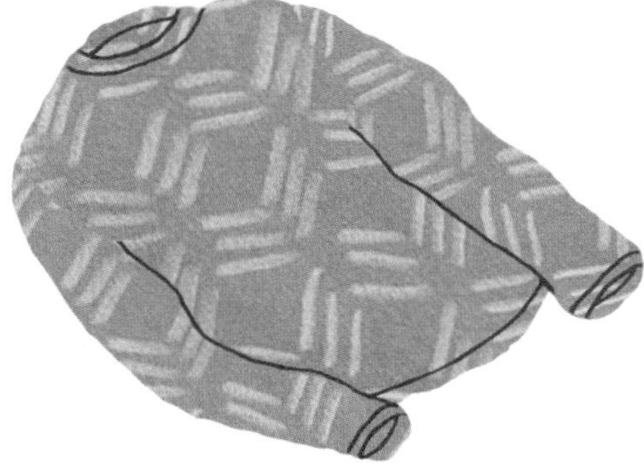

Another way to encourage a shift in perspective is to simply change our physical position. Inversions like forward folds or headstands place our head below our heart—and sometimes that reversal is just what we need.

Lying on a bed or couch (or if you're feeling daring, a park bench), let your head hang off the edge so that you're looking at the world upside down. If a hand- or headstand or "crow" pose is accessible to you, try that instead. Settle into your inverted position for a few minutes, or for as long as it's comfortable, allowing your eyes to trick your brain into seeing the ceiling as the floor and vice versa. As you return to an upright position, track what may have changed. Has a "stuck" thought shaken loose?

If you're feeling unsettled or anxious, notice how your clothing feels on your body. Is your waistband restricting your belly? Is the collar of your sweater itchy? Are your shoes pinching your toes? Even though we tolerate these minor discomforts, our clothes influence our physical experience, which in turn affects our mind and outlook. And like the adventure sweaters, particular garments have the power to bring out qualities we want to embody. If you wish to be more playful, for example, favor clothes in your closet that draw out this quality in you. Experiment with changing clothes when you crave a shift in energy.

My grandma used to say that whenever she was feeling worried, she would pick up a broom and start to sweep. Small tasks around the house are purposeful and rewarding, and busying ourselves with physical work can be an excellent way to reorient a worrying mind. If you're feeling stuck, look around your home and notice what needs attention. A drawer stuffed with old papers? A disorganized cabinet? Add a plant, open a window, move furniture around. Decluttering, cleaning, or even just reimagining your physical space can open channels you might not have realized were blocked, allowing for more flow in other parts of your life as well.

no endings
no beginnings

the big circle

A friend of mine gave birth to her son in the living room of her rental home. Shortly thereafter, her neighbor shared with her that the house's previous resident—an elderly man—had died in the very same room. Wherever we stand on this earth, many, many others have stood before. The land is layered with stories, and an infinity of beings, human and more-than-human alike, inform its texture.

I try to listen carefully to what my children tell me. Because they're so young, I believe they're closer to "the source"—our spiritual place of origin. So when my older daughter was three years old and asking big "why" questions, I would often respond, "I'm not sure. What do you think?" The answers she gave were profound. At three, she was just beginning to comprehend the notion of death but did not seem particularly afraid of it. "It's a big circle," she said once, as though this were entirely obvious, and drew a circle in the air in front of her.

This makes sense. So much in nature is cyclical. The cycle of the seasons mirrors that of our lifetimes, spring being our birth and infancy, summer our youth, autumn our adulthood, and winter our elderhood. Birth and death exist at the same point on the circle, where winter ends and spring begins anew. My parents, who were with my grandmother as she was dying, said the process looked remarkably like birth. Although we perceive our lives to exist along a linear, one-dimensional track, in many ways, as we enter old age, we're simply circling back.

Are endings truly endings? Are beginnings really beginnings? Thich Nhat Hanh, the great Buddhist spiritual teacher, once consoled a grieving child, comparing her lost loved one to a beautiful cloud that had become rain. "Your beloved one continues always," he said. When we look deeply, we see that there is no real death—only transformation. We fear the disintegration of self that we think death entails, but what if death is actually an integration (or reintegration)? A merging with lichen and ginkgo and cloudcap, with raven and rushing river. A wholeness like we've never experienced before.

While we often fear and resist change, we can practice viewing it peacefully. Find a smooth stone at least the size of your palm. Dip a paintbrush (or your finger) in water and paint intuitively on the stone's surface. Watch the drawing drip and shape-shift in surprising ways, ultimately dissolving within minutes to form a blank canvas. As your drawing fades, remind yourself that it is making way for the next beautiful iteration.

Close your eyes and visualize your birth. Who was there? Birth can look so many different ways, but most of us are born into protective arms: those of a parent, a midwife, a nurse or physician. Imagine if your birth—your entrance into this world—also meant your exit from another. If that were so, we might reframe death as a beginning. Imagine how it would feel, upon your death, to be delivered into the protective arms of ancestors and loved ones who went before you. The same way you were received at your birth. Who might be there? What might it look like?

In her book *From Here to Eternity*, the mortician and writer Caitlin Doughty describes how the Torajan people of remote Indonesia see the boundary between life and death as permeable. Family members who have died might be thought of as sick or asleep, maintaining some sensory awareness. Spend half an hour researching other cultures' beliefs about what happens when we die. Seek out perspectives that challenge what your own culture has taught you. Alternatively, try initiating a conversation about death with a friend or family member. Ask your loved ones what they believe. The answers you hear may surprise or inspire you.

the earth holds us

our original home

When my younger daughter was a baby, I quickly discovered that one of the only ways to soothe her during bouts of crying was to go outside. Like water dousing a fire, the fresh air immediately calmed her. Her eyes would widen; her shoulders would relax. Was it the cool air, the wren's song, the dark branches against a bright sky, or a distant train whistle that soothed her? Or was it just that she felt more at home outside than in? Sometimes, I would take off her socks and shoes and place her bare feet down on the grass and dirt. I did this intuitively, recalling the many times I had found comfort in nature's embrace.

Once, while attending a conference with many older, more experienced professionals, I used a break between sessions to visit the woods. I had been feeling shy and self-conscious, unsure of my own worthiness, so I went where I knew I could be fully myself. As I took my place among the trees and birds and insects, I sensed Mother Earth's unconditional acceptance. After a few moments,

I walked back into the workshop feeling grounded and peaceful, and all day I carried with me a powerful sense of belonging.

For millennia, our ancestors spent most of their time outside, in fog and wind, ice and rain. Only in relatively recent history have we begun living almost completely indoors. Our ancestors bathed in cool rivers, warmed their feet in thermal pools, filled their eyes with the sights of thunderheads and fleeting rainbows; they picked fat, delicious berries directly from bushes and ate the freshest fish imaginable.

Thousands of years spent communing with the wild are still deeply embedded in us, and many of our modern anxieties spring from a lack of connection to the elements that make us whole. This yearning might be hidden or unconscious, but we experience it when we can't sit still at our work desks, when we crack a window and the outside air rushes in, awakening something ancient within us. This is what is seeding, or stoking, our agitation: a separation from the expansive sky, the streaming rain, the morning sunlight, and from everyday encounters with foxes and woodchucks and songbirds. On the surface, we may be comforted by the LED beams that flood our homes at night, but deep down, our eyes long to drink starlight and firelight. Something in us misses the dappled shadows on the forest floor, the embers drifting up to the heavens. We've sacrificed much more than we realize.

Gather a bit of dirt or sand from a place that holds meaning for you, preferably a place where you've felt at home. Put it in a glass jar and keep it somewhere easily accessible, such as on an altar or shelf. In times of stress or worry, take this jar down, open it, touch the soil or sand, or spill it out into the palm of your hand. Close your eyes and call up the comforting feelings that come with being in that special place.

Seize every opportunity to go outside during the day. When you take the trash out, linger for a few extra moments. When you go to the grocery store, pause in the parking lot to feel the sun on your face. Find some time during your evening to walk around barefoot outdoors, like a young child. Feel the soil, the grass woven between your toes. Walk on a muddy path. Rest in a patch of grass and feel the earth rising up to support you. Gently press your palm to moss, or bring a smooth stone or fallen leaf to your cheek. Run your fingers along a tree's bark. Kneel in a garden and bury your nose in the humus. Do these things especially when you feel ungrounded, dysregulated, or out of control. Let the land hold you tenderly, soothing you as only a parent can.

Words have an incantatory power, especially nature words. With them, we can conjure the magic of the natural world, even when we can't physically access it. Explore your own natural vocabulary, and identify words that soothe. Whisper or speak them aloud: "yarrow," "chickweed," "comfrey," "warbler," "kestrel." Or, if you can access the outdoors, practice naming the plants and animals and stones you come across in your yard or on a walk. Look up their names if you don't already know them. Let the music of these words be an invocation.

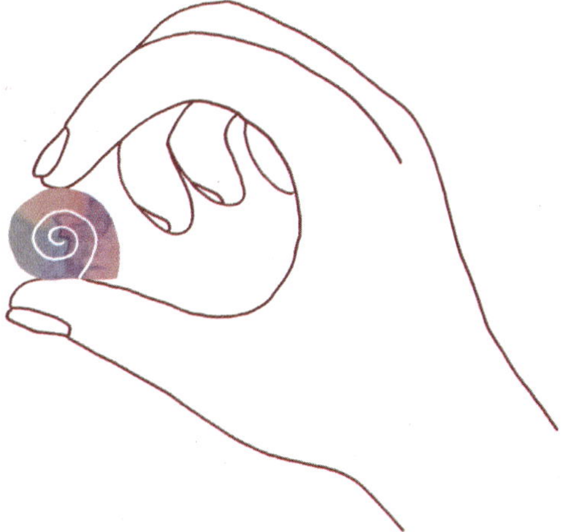

LET
EVERYTHING
BE A
TEACHER

snakebite teachings

What if the difficult people in our lives were actually spiritual masters inviting our evolution? Perhaps the condescending boss is teaching you to use your voice to stand up for yourself. Maybe the person taking forever at the checkout counter is inviting you to cultivate more patience. One of the wisest things someone said to me when I was in the thick of parenting two tough-as-nails small children was, "Ah, lucky you, you have two tiny gurus." Learning to see my children as my greatest spiritual teachers changed everything for me. I came to experience the challenges of being a new parent—the getting up multiple times in the middle of the night, the high-decibel tantrums and sibling fights—as invitations to mature as a person, to grow alongside my daughters.

We can choose some of our teachers in this life, but many times, our teachers choose us. My friend Monique was once bitten by a copperhead snake. The recovery was grueling, rendering her bedridden for over three weeks while the swelling in her leg slowly subsided. During this time, she was forced to rely on her roommates and friends for nearly constant help. Previously, she had been reluctant to ask much of others, fearing her needs might be burdensome. To be strong, she thought, she had to do everything for herself. But the snake pushed her into a position of great vulnerability and need, and in this way, it became her teacher. Again and again, she battled discomfort and asked for help—and each time a friend came to her aid, she not only gained trust but she also became more deeply enmeshed in her community.

When we are curious about the lessons our experiences may hold for us, we avoid foundering in self-pity or despair. This isn't to say we should ignore or minimize our anger or grief. In fact, we may need to feel those emotions in order to access what we're being invited to learn. It isn't often a swift or easy process, and it's important to give ourselves grace. But by exploring how even painful experiences can be opportunities for growth, we allow for the possibility of great healing.

As you go about your week, watch for the "snakebite teachings." A disagreement with a friend may illuminate a tendency toward defensiveness. A twisted ankle or cut finger might invite you to reflect on how absentmindedly you move your body. Record these events and how they could help you evolve. Throughout your week (or over a longer period), note each event—"twisted ankle" or "fight with a friend"—on one side of an index card, and on the opposite side, write the possible teaching. Return to these at the end of the week, month, or year, reviewing what you've learned.

The word "teacher" may call to mind the image of a person at the head of a classroom, but teachers can take many forms. Is there a stone that catches your eye on a walk? A bird that keeps visiting your stoop? A poem or song you come back to again and again? Once you identify someone or something as your teacher, listen for what teachings or assignments they might have for you. For instance, if you come across a beautiful and unusual shell on a walk, ask yourself what you were thinking about when you found it. If you spot a snake in the garden, reflect on the qualities snakes possess and how those might relate to what's going on in your life. (For example, a snake's vision clouds while it sheds its skin, rendering it temporarily blind until its transformation is complete. Are you, too, experiencing a period of confusion as you shed limiting beliefs?) Finally, consider that worry itself can be a teacher. While we tend to want to banish it, a recurring worry might show us what needs to change or shift in our lives.

ordinary gifts

Years ago, a friend and I challenged ourselves to a thirty-mile walk through the forest on the winter solstice. As we scampered over fallen logs and slid on icy patches, we fell into trading complaints about which parts of our bodies were achy and numb. It was easy to gripe, but as we gave attention to our discomforts, they only seemed to intensify, making us doubt whether we could go on. At some point along the way, my friend suggested that we share what was feeling good. We acknowledged that our bellies were full, our minds clear, our spirits up. Her back was feeling limber and strong, and my feet were surprisingly warm. We talked about how our shared experience that day was deepening our friendship, how we felt proud of ourselves for pushing our limits.

We tend to focus on what causes us pain: a wounded relationship with a family member, betrayal by a lover, discord in the workplace. These things deserve our attention, our care—but not to the exclusion of all else. Even in the midst of hardship, beauty appears: A friend calls to see how we're doing; a hot shower waits for us on a chilly day; there is food warming in the oven or clean water to drink. Our lives are filled with these ordinary gifts that, if we let them, reveal themselves to be extraordinary.

Close your eyes and mentally "scan" your body from head to toe. Try this in the shower or as you dress for the day. Notice which parts feel at ease, nourished, or content. If you encounter pain or discomfort, don't attempt to avoid or ignore it, but try to meet the sensation with curiosity rather than judgment or fear. Give thanks for all the ways your body works to keep you alive and healthy without your conscious instruction.

If you've spent any time with a baby or young toddler, you'll know that even the simplest things captivate them: water dripping from a faucet, bubbles, crinkly paper. What if, like babies, we viewed our day-to-day life as though for the first time? Might we glimpse the miraculous in the mundane? A few times throughout your day, whisper to yourself, "It's a miracle that . . ." ***It's a miracle that my beloved loves me back. It's a miracle that this dishwasher is doing my dishes. It's a miracle that rain is coming today.*** **Practice looking through this lens and you will gradually awaken to the wonders around you.**

Recall a time in your life when you desperately wanted something that you now have: a skill, a particular job title, a house of your own. Try to remember the visceral yearning you felt for this thing, then reflect on what happened once you obtained it. How did you feel a week, a month, or a year later? Often, our yearning is never satisfied, but it takes new forms. Pause to acknowledge what you've earned, achieved, or been given. Relish in a moment of contentedness.

a widening
of vision
a vision of
widening

expansion

One root of the word "stress" is the Old French *estresse* meaning "narrowness." To release stress, we must sense some kind of expansion in the body or mind—an opening up where something felt closed down, or a broadening of our perspective.

Countless storylines and dramas are unfolding right this minute, everywhere on Earth, yet we are only privy to a tiny fraction of them. There are billions of people on this planet, and each of us has a story, a set of worries and fears. When I'm going through something challenging, I try to remind myself of this. Chances are, many, many others are facing a similar predicament to my own, perhaps even sharing in my worry. This simple reminder widens my view, making me feel less alone in my struggles, and it deepens my compassion for those around me.

A friend of mine visits the wilderness often, he says, to remind himself of his smallness and to try to sense who he is in relation to other beings. In wild places, where we glimpse Earth's geologic timescale in stone formations and river gorges, our day-to-day worries are put in perspective. Undistracted by the demands of modern life, we might notice the vivid animacy of the natural world: a red-tailed hawk hunting overhead, alpine asters decorating the hillside, or even termites devouring a rotting log. Nature consists of a vibrant and intricate network of relationships, and while we are a part of this network, we aren't at its center. This expansion of vision may invite a vision of expansion: Our concept of self may widen and deepen, and we may receive newfound clarity around our purpose in this life.

Lie down on your bed, close your eyes, and try to see yourself and your bedroom as though you were hovering near your ceiling, looking down. Observe your furniture, your belongings; see yourself lying still on the bed. Now zoom out and envision your house or apartment building from above. Picture the roof among other roofs in your community. Fly higher and take in the expansiveness of your region. Note its landmarks receding as you float even higher, eventually reaching outer space. Gaze down at our slowly turning planet. Spend a moment here. From this high-up vantage, our worries may become very small.

Visiting another country is an incredible way to gain perspective on our own lives, but we don't always have the resources or ability to travel. Luckily, an internet connection allows us to explore other parts of the world without leaving home. Think of a place you've wanted to visit. (The Greek islands? Mongolia? Port-au-Prince?) Locate it on Google Earth. Then use the Street View feature to virtually walk the streets of that place. Let your curiosity be your guide. You may be surprised by how lifelike and immersive this experience can be. There's no replacing actual travel, but when that isn't an option, or when you're pressed for time, a simulated "trip" can help you see beyond your small corner of the world.

the unseen among us

Each of us has four grandparents, eight great-grandparents, sixteen great-great-grandparents, thirty-two great-great-great-grandparents, sixty-four great-great-great-great-grandparents, and so on—we have thousands of ancestors. So much had to go right in each person's life, generation after generation, for millennia, to ensure our existence.

Close your eyes and picture your ancestors surrounding you in a great circle. These may be your blood relatives, or they may be your kin in another sense. They are the people who have hoped and sacrificed for you, whose lives have made way for yours. They gaze at you lovingly. Some take turns approaching you, enfolding you in a hug or simply touching your hand or cheek. Remember that each one of these people is still here with you, their bone dust in every living leaf, their souls in sunbeams, murmurations, and the dew on a spider's web. Now imagine the circle around you widening to include your descendants. Even if you don't have or plan to have children, dear ones will carry your words and ways into the future. Somehow, they, too, are here with you now, like latent seeds.

When we feel weak or lost, we can look to these unseen supports—our literal and spiritual ancestors and descendants—to guide us.

Many of us experience death as a rupture, a permanent end to a deep connection. While death certainly involves loss, there are ways to maintain our relationships with loved ones long after their physical bodies have gone. Throughout history and around the world, people have found ways to commune with the dead. Often, this communion takes the form of simple acknowledgment. In many cultures, families dedicate home altars to ancestors. Mexican *ofrendas* traditionally include incense, flowers, and a bit of food the deceased person loved. Japanese butsudans offer rice and water. Prepare a home altar of your own. It can include photos of your loved one, notes from them, or some of their treasured possessions. The first step to rekindling a relationship with the dead is to invite them back into your physical space.

Food is a portal to memory and tradition. A potent way to connect with those who've gone before us is to plan a feast of ancestral foods. Ask relatives for family recipes that have been passed down through the generations, or if that isn't accessible, research the traditional foods associated with your ethnic or cultural heritage. Ask your friends or neighbors to do the same, and come together for a potluck. Remember to honor the ancestors by making a plate for them; fill it with a small portion of each dish before serving yourself.

At points in my artistic career when I've faced a creative block or worried about the reception of a new piece, I've looked for guidance from ancestors who were artists and writers. When I've struggled as a mother, I've sought the support of my ancestral matriarchs—especially my grandma Sara, who mothered five children. Choose one ancestor and ask for their help with a specific worry. Use their name and speak to them aloud. Explain the situation in detail; articulating it may help you clarify it for yourself. If it feels more appropriate to talk to a future descendant, try that instead. A friend of mine used to speak with her future child, imploring him to help her find his father (the partner she had not met yet). And I have spoken to my descendants when deep in worry about the state of our earth. Get curious about making a connection, experiment with it, and watch what unfolds; you may uncover a fountain of support you never knew existed.

darkness illuminates

For the Celts, the day traditionally began at dusk, not dawn. This makes sense when we remember that seeds germinate underground and babies gestate in a dark womb for nine months before bursting forth into the light. While darkness tends to elicit fear in us, it can be supportive—a place of growth and transformation.

According to the mythologist and storyteller Joseph Campbell, "the very cave you are afraid to enter turns out to be the source of what you are looking for." When you enter a literal cave, at first you see nothing but darkness. A sense of panic might set in as your eyes dart around trying to make out shapes. The cave asks you to surrender, to make peace with not knowing. The cave is your covenant with mystery. If you linger there long enough, in the uncomfortable darkness, your eyes will eventually adjust, and you will begin to see hints of light. These illuminations are Truth, which is often quiet and subtle and which can only emerge when we've committed to and accepted the darkness.

Our fears usually stem from a reluctance to lose the things or people we hold dear. But surrendering to the darkness requires us to let go, and in doing so, we learn to love more fully. Our darkest worries and fears can reveal what really matters to us. The inevitabilities of death and change that underlie so much anxiety can bring the present moment, with all its gifts, into vivid focus, prompting joy and lending an air of preciousness to our interactions.

Have you ever dreamt of your own or a loved one's death? Dreams like these can be a gift, because life takes on a new poignancy in the hours or even days to follow. Imagine if you learned that today would be your last. How would that change how you perceive your current worries? Where would you spend your time and with whom? What would come into focus? Write these details down or, better yet, make good on them: Share a truth with someone; indulge in your favorite things; feel the sacredness of the present moment.

Journal about what you would like to be able to say at the end of a long life. How do you hope to reflect back on your experiences? How would you like people to remember you? Contemplating these questions can help you identify what's most important to you, and it can push you to live according to your values.

Challenge your fears around death by listening to the stories of loved ones who've attended the dying or by absorbing firsthand accounts of near-death experiences. (You can begin by browsing the archives of the Near-Death Experience Research Foundation.) Many of these stories are incredible: They include frequent mention of golden light, beautiful gardens, reunions with friends and relatives who've gone before, and an overwhelming sense of peace. Whatever we believe about death, these accounts can be illuminating, and they can help us feel more curious and less afraid.

allowing
trying

effort and ease

A few days before I gave birth to my first child, my mother-in-law, a practicing yogi for decades, offered me the ancient principle of Sthira Sukha. *Sthira* is Sanskrit for "steadiness" or "effort," and *Sukha* means "comfort" or "ease." She shared that, in each yoga pose, effort and ease should be held in balance. When I went into labor, I kept this in mind. If I strained too much, I would tire myself out well before I reached the finish line. Despite the excitement, I had to let myself truly rest after a contraction, in order to store up energy for the next. But if I relaxed completely, my labor might stall. I tried to listen closely for when my body was telling me to fire up and put in extra effort and when it was asking me to surrender and ride the waves with ease.

There is an art to balancing action with inaction. When we ride a bike, we pedal when we need to and then coast when we can. To ride far, we must do both things well. But many of us tend to favor one strategy over the other. The same is true when it comes to anxiety.

When we are worried about something, some of us throw ourselves into action, trying to control the outcome through an outpouring of energy. Others are paralyzed by fear or indecision and do nothing at all. By exerting too much effort, we invite disappointment and burnout, but by being too easeful, we risk standing still. Finding balance looks like putting in the work while simultaneously letting go and trusting in the process.

In what areas of your life could you pedal more, and in what areas could you coast? What is your natural inclination or tendency—trying hard or allowing? Can you strike a balance? Find a physical activity that requires balancing effort and ease—such as riding a bike, swimming, yoga, or even walking. Notice how the relationship between effort and ease creates harmony and how moving our bodies can settle our minds.

Aligning our actions with the lunar cycle can teach us when our efforts will be most effective and when we are better off resting. The new moon is a time for turning inward, resting and reflecting, and visualizing new beginnings. The waxing moon is a time for taking actionable steps toward those visions. At the full moon, we may be compelled to take what we've been working on and share it with others or to make what is in our hearts visible. Waning moon energy is good for purging and cleansing, for releasing anything that has been weighing on us. During the waning moon, we may also focus on wrapping up any lingering projects. Experiment with structuring your month and year according to the lunar cycle. This could look like scheduling a presentation around the full moon or planning a restful retreat during a new moon. See if things feel more balanced when your efforts are aligned with natural rhythms.

In our fast-paced, productivity-obsessed culture, we tend to undervalue rest. Even if we succeed in balancing effort with ease, it can be difficult to escape the sense that time spent resting is time "wasted." Humans are unique in this way; other animals seem to accept that rest serves an essential purpose. Consider the spider, for example. With great effort, she weaves her complex web. Then, she must wait in stillness. Not only does this period of rest give her time to recharge but it also means her potential prey won't be startled by her movements. Before you enter an intentional period of rest, consider its purpose. Understand that, by sitting in stillness, you honor your past efforts and ensure their effectiveness.

LOOK FOR
THE LIGHT

becoming heliotropic

Heliotropic plants, like daisies, poppies, and sunflowers, continually face the sun as it arcs across the sky. When darkness falls, these plants orient east, awaiting the next sunrise. We, too, can grow toward the light, seeking and finding it in every situation.

On a trip to California a few years ago, my partner and I visited a friend of his parents, John, who had been paralyzed from the waist down in a boogie-boarding accident. Despite this, he was the most upbeat, always-on-the-verge-of-riotous-laughter person I'd ever met. He frequently led jam sessions on guitar and volunteered at a local preschool as a music teacher. Beloved by many, John had a vivacity and thirst for life rarely found in those who have *not* experienced such hardship. Meeting John opened my eyes to the human capacity for joy—our extraordinary ability to find the light—even in the most difficult of circumstances.

In his account of surviving the concentration camps, the Jewish psychologist Viktor Frankl recalled fellow prisoners who comforted others or gave away their last pieces of bread. For Frankl, these people were exercising what he called "the last of the human freedoms." While we may have little to no control over what happens to us in life, we can always "choose [our] own way"—that is, choose how we orient to our circumstances. What's more, in finding a way to accept what cannot be changed and bear our burden with dignity, we model the resilience of the human spirit for others.

Often, when we're anxious, it can feel as though we have no choice but to worry. This sense of powerlessness is usually false; in actuality, we can choose whether to feed or starve our fears. Start by sensing the physical cues that tell you when worry is setting in. Perhaps your heart rate speeds up. Maybe your palms sweat or you pick at the skin around your fingernails. When you spot one of these cues, practice pausing to name what you're experiencing. Speak it aloud: "I am worrying. Hello, worry." Now that you've observed and greeted your worry, you can see that it is separate from you—a passing thought. You can choose whether to invite it in or send it away.

In a heated conversation, it can be easy to react emotionally and impulsively, sometimes in ways we later regret. But even in these moments of fiery back-and-forth, we have a choice. Some Buddhists practice pausing for a full minute before responding in conversation, but even a few seconds of silence can lead to a more mindful reply. The next time you're having an emotional exchange, consciously pause before speaking. Let your emotions settle. Ask yourself if what you are about to say is what you really mean.

Facing a daunting series of medical treatments, my friend Anna resolved to look for the light in her situation. The hospital was in a vibrant city neighborhood, so she made a point to explore it after her appointments. Anna took time to get to know her fellow patients and the hospital staff, many of whom she befriended and looked forward to seeing. She says her time in treatment deepened her capacity for love in a way she hopes will never wane. Of course, the experience was still difficult, but it was made more tolerable by Anna's outlook.

Think of an ongoing challenge you're facing—perhaps you're stressed by a project at work or struggling with parenthood or finances. First, remind yourself that this is temporary; you won't always feel this way. Then, without diminishing the hardship at hand, can you resolve to look for the light around its edges? In your journal, list the small but meaningful gifts of your situation. Writing these down may help magnify them in your mind.

helping heals

a retired pastor, my grandpa Gene lived out his final years in the memory ward of a senior home. Even as he suffered from dementia and declining health, he continued to minister to others. Each time I visited, I'd find him holding a different resident's hand, nodding silently while they spoke or simply offering his presence. It was beautiful to see him in his element despite his illness—and to know that these interactions were medicine for him too.

In a culture that idolizes independence, many of us hesitate to ask for help in times of struggle. We may assume that we are inconveniencing others, but often, when we ask for someone's assistance, we are giving that person the opportunity to feel needed. Personally, I am honored when someone calls me for advice. Cooking a meal for a friend in need fills me with satisfaction. These are invitations to feel deliciously purposeful.

We are communal beings; the knowledge that others have our back is crucial to our health, and so is a sense that we are needed. Look around and you will find someone for whom service offers fulfillment. The trusted friend. The beloved aunt. Even a kind stranger. Allow yourself to be helped, and also open yourself to the pleasure inherent in helping others.

Have you ever asked someone for something and been surprised to receive it? A raise at work? An extension on a homework assignment? Forgiveness for a wrong you've done? There is a human being on the other side of your question who likely understands how challenging life can be. Expressing what we want or need is powerful medicine. What is one area of your life in which you could really use some help right now? Is it getting organized? Is it managing your back pain? Is it processing a difficult interaction? Pinpoint one thing and identify who you'll reach out to for support.

I was once part of an ask-and-offer circle—around ten people who got together regularly to express current needs and respond to those of others in the group. I was in awe of how frequently asks were fulfilled—for example, someone shared that their bicycle had been stolen and they needed a new one; another person in the group offered the spare in their garage. Someone else needed a friend with whom to talk through a problem; almost immediately, a hand went up with an offer to listen. No need was too big or too small.

Organize an ask-and-offer circle of your own. Gather a group that meets regularly, or install a bulletin board in a public space (a local coffee shop, church, school, or food co-op) on which folks can post what they need or what they can give. You may be surprised by the generosity of your community.

Prayer is an ancient and powerful tool we can use to unburden ourselves of our worries and feel supported. Through prayer, we can speak candidly about our concerns. Many people assume that prayer must be formal, that it must involve a script, or that it's only appropriate in a religious context. I prefer to think of prayer as a conversation with a loving, unseen guide. While a prayer might address Allah, Krishna, God, Creator, Mother Mary, or Pachamama—it doesn't need to involve a deity. A prayer might address the spirit of a tree or stone or body of water; it might speak to a beloved ancestor or "the ancestors" in general. You may feel connected to a particular saint, to angels, or to house spirits. The important thing is that you feel supported by the entity you address. They may not respond overtly, but you sense they are listening. Some people like to establish a special place or time in which to pray, while others pray whenever they yearn for support, wherever they happen to be. Like setting down a heavy burden or finally sharing its weight, prayer can offer immense relief.

the hand we wish to hold

Walking is essentially a process of falling and catching ourselves, thousands of times per day. Each step carries a risk, a possibility of failure, yet we instinctively learn to steady ourselves, trusting our bodies to keep us upright. When I feel like I'm losing my footing, I rely on the knowledge I've gathered to keep moving forward. Sometimes, this means reaching out for help. But often, with a great deal of self-compassion, I can summon the soothing I need from within.

Once, when I was very sick and in the emergency room, a nurse placed a heated blanket over me. Her simple gesture brought instant comfort. Since then, I've adopted the practice of wrapping myself or a family member in a favorite wool blanket—the "magic healing blanket"—when one of us is feeling anxious or unwell. Swaddled in its warmth, we feel steadied in space, held, and protected.

Each of us has our own way of soothing ourselves. A friend carries a stone in his pocket, which calms him when he touches it throughout the day. Another friend releases the day's stress by unraveling her braids and brushing her hair out each evening. My five-year-old daughter, who worries a lot at night, has a tiny stuffed elephant she traces along her cheek to help her fall asleep. "I'm contenting myself," she tells me.

Many of our best tools for coping with anxiety are already within us—and each one is a custom fit. We know best what contents us, how to find our footing when we're unstable. We can be our own counsel, the hand we wish to hold.

Sometimes, a single word is all we need to hear. Its specificity and directness can orient us. A few years ago, my friend Reed affixed a sign reading "APPLAUSE" above his stairs, where he and his family would see it each morning. That one word was enough to elicit a feeling of accomplishment, suggesting that simply getting out of bed in this broken world is an action worthy of praise. What word or short phrase could serve as an orienting touchstone for you? Perhaps it's a verb, like "simplify" or "connect," or maybe it's a noun—a quality you wish to cultivate. I recently wrote the word "PATIENCE" on a piece of paper above my desk. Whenever I glance up from my work, especially in a moment of frustration, the word steadies me, reminding me to trust the process. Think of the word you need to hear, write it down, and display it in your home where you'll see it often.

Write a letter to yourself as though you were comforting a friend or parenting a child. What would you tell your friend? How would you soothe your beloved child? Alternatively, speak aloud to yourself as though you were your own counselor. What advice or comfort would you give someone in your situation? Take this practice a step further and record yourself speaking these reassuring words. Replay them as often as you need.

◎

When I was little, my family and I went to Canada each summer to camp near the shores of Lake Huron. We would wait to visit the beach until midday, when the round stones that covered the ground had been warmed by the sun. Then we'd lay down on blankets and place the stones on each other's backs. I remember the sensation of tension melting away, as though the stones were absorbing my stress. We didn't know it then, but we were practicing the ancient healing art of hot stone therapy.

To try this yourself, find a few smooth, round stones about the size of your palm. These can be river rocks, beach stones, or stones from the earth. Leave them in a sunny spot on a warm day, or heat them in the oven. (Two to three minutes at 200 to 275 degrees Fahrenheit should do the trick.) Once heated, handle the stones with tongs or potholders. Gently tap one with your fingertip to test its warmth, then try holding it in your palm. If you can't do this comfortably for five seconds, briefly place the stone under cool water before trying it in your palm again. Once the stones have reached a comfortable temperature, place them on your body, either directly on your skin or atop clothing or a sheet. Arrange them on your legs, belly, or face, or have someone place them on your back. Visualize the stones drawing any tension up and out of your body. Perhaps ask the stones to absorb your worries, or repeat one of these mantras:

> ***"Like this stone, I warm the world with my touch."***
> ***"This stone reminds me who I am."***
> ***"Let this stone's ancient memory guide me."***

When you're finished, return the stones to their home outdoors.

WHILE
YOU
LIVE,
SHINE

the queen of the night

Deep in the woods, the song of my friend Daniel's flute melds with that of the chickadees overhead. Orange sassafras leaves fall softly at Daniel's feet as he plays the oldest known complete musical composition in the world, the Seikilos epitaph. A Greek inscription sourced from the ancient town of Tralles in present-day Turkey, the composition is around two thousand years old:

While you live, shine
have no grief at all
life exists only for a short while
and Time demands an end.

The song makes me think of the illustrious Queen of the Night—a cactus that blooms only once a year, from dusk until the following dawn, but whose fragrance is so intoxicating and whose flowers are so breathtaking, people travel from far and wide to witness its brief flourishing. Perhaps the author of the Seikilos epitaph was memorializing someone who, like the Queen of the Night, shined brightly, if briefly.

We are often advised to "live in the moment," but that is easier said than done: Many of us spend the present worrying incessantly about the past and future, rehashing old troubles and imagining scenarios that may never come to pass. The inscription urges us to consider whether this fretting is a good use of our brief and precious time on Earth. "Time demands an end," the author reminds us, which is to say: Life is fleeting. When we accept the inevitability of our death, we remember to live fully.

Truthfully, few of us will live entirely in the present, nor will we always shine like the Queen of the Night. But the hope these lyrics convey, our striving toward this ideal, are part of what makes us human.

Daniel tells me he sings the Seikilos epitaph to his two-year-old son, José, as a lullaby. Just the other day, he was pleased to hear José singing it softly to himself, expressing an ancient yearning he intuitively understands.

Begin to notice when you are worrying about the past or future. When an uncomfortable memory arises, ask yourself whether it is useful to think about. If no, make a decision to let it go, saying, "I release all attachment to the unchangeable past." Then bring yourself back into the moment by narrating what is happening: "I'm drinking this delicious tea, which is warming me with nourishing herbs." When you find yourself worrying about the future, try saying aloud, "The future is not yet written," and return to the moment again by describing it: "I am sweeping the floor of my house, which shelters me from the rain and cold."

Think back to a time when you were very worried about something, only to have the situation turn out fine. It's likely you've experienced this many times—and that's because we tend to worry over what hasn't happened yet, which, much of the time, never does. Framed this way, worry is rarely worth the stress it brings. Even when your worry does prove justified, the worry itself did nothing to change the outcome. Sometimes, this reminder of the futility of worry is enough to dissipate it or at least put it in perspective.

At least once a day, I like to call to mind this advice from a teacher of mine: "Pause what you're doing and take the deepest breath you've taken all day." Our breath is a powerful tool for hitching ourselves to the present moment. When you find yourself worrying, breathe in through your nose for seven counts, then exhale through your mouth for eleven counts, emptying your diaphragm completely. Breathe deeply from your belly and not shallowly in your throat. Place your hands on your abdomen to feel it rising and falling. Lengthening your exhales in this way signals to your body that you are safe. Even when you're free from worry, you can nourish your nervous system by bringing these deep, elongated breaths into your daily rhythm. Try breathing this way while you're stopped at a red light or as you wash your hands.

WE SHAPE
OUR REALITY

the forest sprite

A few months ago, during a phone call with my mom, she shared the mishaps of her week: The plumbing backed up and flooded the basement, the car broke down, and she lost her favorite bracelet. Yet, instead of sounding frustrated, she seemed a little amused. "A forest sprite is playing tricks on me!" she laughed. As a children's book maker and lover of stories, my mom's childlike spirit is alive. She sees playful figures and faces in everything—from electrical gadgets to morning oatmeal and stray bits of string on the floor. I chuckled at the notion of a forest sprite causing her troubles, but it dawned on me that her perspective helped her to feel less frustrated and more at ease. Consciously or not, she was reframing her experience to avoid unnecessary worry.

The way we frame things significantly shapes our reality. My husband's writer friend, for instance, never resents getting a cold; he actually values being sick for the altered state of mind it brings, which fuels his craft. During a lengthy job search, another friend reframed her rejections as redirections that brought her closer to her ideal role. We often worry about getting older, but what if we reframed aging as a beautiful maturation, an initiation into wise elderhood? Reframing our perspective enables us to begin to make peace with the inevitabilities of life rather than resisting them.

It takes practice to unravel habitual thinking patterns, and learning to reframe is no exception. Start by relying on language to shift your perspective. Notice the difference between saying, "I have to wake up early to exercise," and "I get to wake up early to exercise." Practice replacing your "have tos" with "get tos" and notice how that feels. Consider whether certain words in your vocabulary support a mindset you wish to shed. Write these in your journal alongside alternatives that feel more aligned.

Gratitude is a powerful tool for reframing our anxieties. When my sister moved into a house near the airport, she couldn't help but worry that a low-flying plane might crash into her home. Each time a jet came in for landing, her anxiety would spike—until she began using gratitude to reframe her thoughts. "Thank you, plane, for getting those passengers home safely," she'd say, or, "Thank you for allowing people to travel quickly and safely." Think of a worry that frequently arises for you. Can you find a way to meet it with gratitude the next time it comes up?

At the end of the day, make a "did-it" list as a refreshing alternative to the morning to-do list. On this list, jot down all the things you did during the day that weren't work related or "productive" but were meaningful acts of care, embodiment, healing, love, or joy. For example, your list might include: "Made myself a healthy lunch. Left a loving voicemail for my dad. Played a game with my daughter." The "did-it" list expands the concept of achievement to include the ways we nourish ourselves and others. Although our days are often filled with these activities, they are seldom documented or acknowledged.

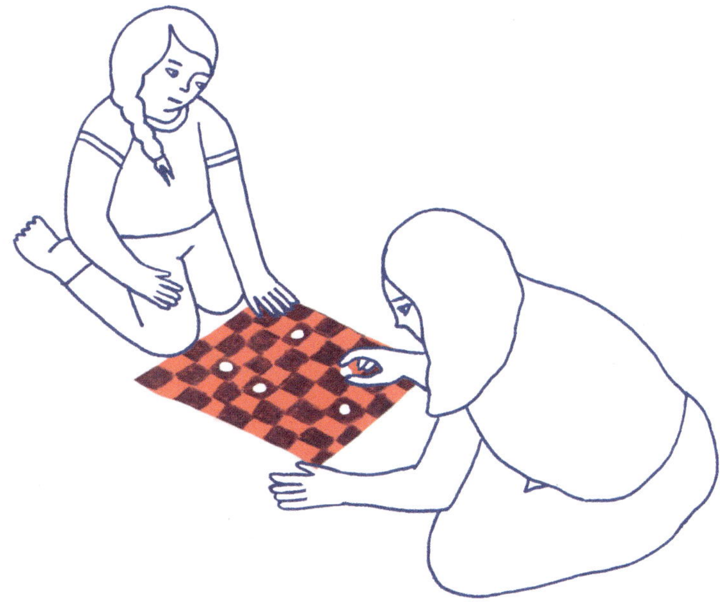

we are
decorated
by
our
stories

dress the wounds in colorful yarns

i grew up watching my pa fix things. Instead of trying to restore something to its perfect, original form, he especially loved to highlight the repair: Our broken refrigerator door handle was replaced with a carved wooden one; our torn window screen was mended with bright-red thread. He taught me to be resourceful, and I learned to mend my clothes. Now, my daughters bring me their socks and leggings when they snag a hole. "Mama, mend it!" they say, and I fill the holes with colorful yarns. My girls wear these mends like badges of honor.

I don't know of a word in English for the feeling of satisfaction, which for me verges on elation, that results from fixing something broken—and yet our culture is not one of repair. We're quick to throw things out, replacing damaged items with new ones. But we humans are not meant to consume and dispose on repeat. We are meant to be healers, creators, full participants in making the world more beautiful and more whole. Our spirits suffer when we stifle this innate creative, healing instinct. Fixing something is like making sweet applesauce out of bruised apples; the thing is made better by the attention of our hands. What's more, when we busy these hands with care, panic subsides and the mind clears. In this space of peaceful productivity, we can take a deep breath.

Just like scars on a body, every mend in a garment tells a story. *This is where my sleeve snagged on a bramble that day we took a walk through the fog. This is where my pant leg ripped, riding my bike to the potluck where we met.* The scars from old wounds, the mends in a beloved garment, they all say: I have truly lived.

Inspect your clothes for holes to mend. If you're new to sewing, seek out a simple patching tutorial online or in a book. If you already know how to patch, explore mending techniques you haven't yet mastered: plain weave, Swiss, or Scotch darning. Research how to repair a broken zipper. Mending is problem-solving, and learning to successfully mend clothing can boost your confidence in other areas. How might a repair mindset apply to less tangible snags or problems in your life?

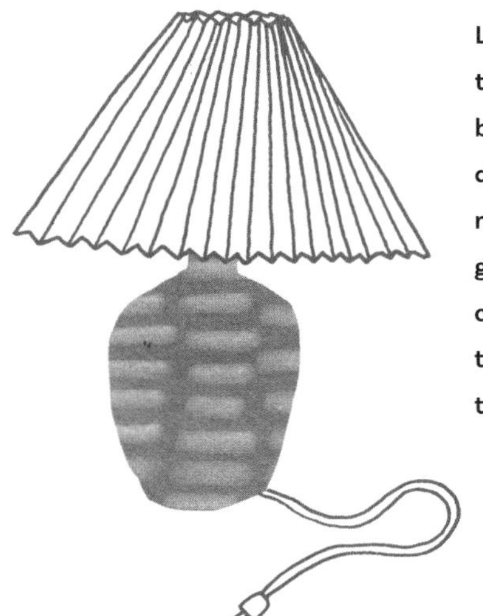

Look around your house for more, beyond clothing, that needs repair. Does your bedside lamp need its bulb replaced? Have you been tolerating a busted door hinge? A sticky dresser drawer? These things may seem minor, but if we let them fester, they will get under our skin. Chaos in our external environment can produce the same internally. By taking the time to tend to what's broken in our homes, we restore flow to blocked energy and create more ease for ourselves.

Think twice before throwing things away. Imagine how your "trash" might be repurposed and given new life. Old, threadbare T-shirts and sheets can be cut into strips and braided into rag rugs; broken dish shards can be saved and reused as tiles in a mosaic. A second chance is powerful medicine. It is a recognition of the value inherent in all things, an invitation to greater patience and ingenuity. Now apply this thinking to your relationships, your creative life. Perhaps the dormant friendship is worth renewing, the "ruined" art project worth transforming. Keep track of your discarded ideas, your attempts, and once some time has passed, give them another look.

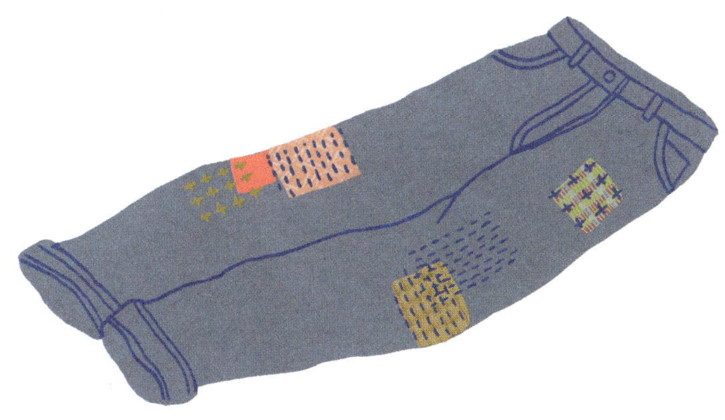

gather
strength

initiation into the mysteries

My sister and I watched as the bus disappeared down the dusty road, taking with it our last tethers to the comforts of civilization. With excitement, nervous anticipation, and backpacks stuffed with camping gear, we turned to face the expansive taiga of Denali National Park in the Alaskan Interior. Resplendent with larch trees, blueberry shrubs, and braided rivers, the park's six million acres are bisected by a single road and no trails. When you leave the road behind, you are truly adrift in a vast wilderness.

On the bus ride in, we spotted several grizzly bears grazing on blueberries and lumbering alongside streams. Before boarding, we'd been required to attend a training about what to do when (not if) we encountered one while hiking. Just days ahead of our trip, for the first time in many years, a bear had attacked a visitor, so while the landscape was dazzling and we were on the adventure of a lifetime, the threat of a bear attack was never far from our minds.

To help calm our nerves, my sister had carved each of us a small wooden bear to carry as a talisman, a protective charm. Whenever I felt anxious, I reached into my pocket to gather strength from the bear. I didn't exactly believe that holding my talisman would ward off the real bears. Rather, touching it helped me feel more connected to them, in all their magic and mystery. If there were to be an encounter, I thought, maybe it could be one filled with wonder rather than fear.

The word "talisman" derives from the Arabic for "charm": *tilsam*. *Tilsam*, in turn, can be traced to the Ancient Greek verb *telein*, which means "to initiate into the mysteries." A talisman—an object imbued with meaning—can put us in touch with the more-than-human realm, growing our connectivity and strengthening our sense of belonging within the rich web of life.

Make or find a talisman to accompany you through challenging times. This could be a stone, an acorn, a gem, or a scrap of fabric—any object that holds meaning for you. Carry this charm in your pocket or wear it on a necklace that rests over your heart. Touch it throughout your day or whenever you're feeling anxious. Notice its steadying effect. Can you draw strength from it?

Like the wooden bear my sister gave me, a gifted talisman is imbued with the giver's love and support. Gift a talisman to a friend or family member who is going through a hard time, or agree to exchange talismans with someone you love. Make a simple ceremony of naming each talisman's purpose.

Ask whether your family members (especially your elders) have any talismans, good-luck charms, or inherited symbols related to protection or strength. Adopt one of these for yourself.

an infinity of stories

One afternoon, my four-year-old daughter burst in to tell me about the balloons she'd seen children releasing on the playground. She loved watching the colorful balls lift up, polka-dotting the sky until they were so tiny they disappeared completely. Where were they going? Her question called to mind photos I'd seen of birds entangled in balloon ribbons, colorful latex bits extracted from the bellies of sea turtles. I almost said, "The balloons will come down and land in a tree or lake, possibly harming an animal, and wherever they land, they will never decompose." But something made me pause. Although I felt an urge to tell her the truth, I also didn't want to drain the magic from her world. She had just witnessed something beautiful.

Sometimes I wish I could unsee the harm in a simple balloon sailing upward into the sky. But the truth is that I don't need to; I can hold the story of the balloon's harm alongside the story of its beauty. Both are equally valid and true. And these aren't the only stories.

Someone else might see a balloon and be reminded of a beloved grandparent, or another might cringe in anticipation of its loud *pop*.

Stories come at us from all angles, all day, often through our screens. They have the power to steer our minds and hearts, stoke our fears, and ultimately shape the way we see the world. When we encounter a sorrowful story, we can practice finding the beauty within or alongside it. We can practice choosing which stories to shed and which to keep, braiding those into our personal cosmology.

Observe what stories enter your world today and how they make you feel. Maybe you hear or read about an act of violence or willful neglect. You may taste a sourness in your mouth, a rising distrust of those around you. Instead of resting there, challenge yourself to look for evidence of another story—one that affirms the goodness of humanity. You might notice the compassionate way your teacher speaks to you after class or your father's generosity as he gives you advice over the phone. Maybe you take a moment to acknowledge those who, decades ago, protected a bit of forest near your town, preserving it for future generations.

Remember that seeking the good in a given situation, or looking for positive narratives in general, is not the same as avoiding difficult feelings or ignoring stories that disturb us. It's important to make room for both, honoring the multiplicity at the heart of our world.

Storytelling is central to the human experience; all day long, we tell stories about ourselves and others, narrating what we think is happening. But our stories aren't always based on facts. Take five minutes to write down what's worrying you. What is the central fear? If you're worried others are criticizing you, describe in detail what you fear may be true. (For example: "My coworkers are talking behind my back. They think I'm not good at my job.") When the time is up, look back at what you wrote. Sentence by sentence, question whether your statements are provably true or based on assumptions. If you're assuming a lot about a situation, it's unlikely you're perceiving it accurately. Challenge yourself to gather more information before spinning a tale.

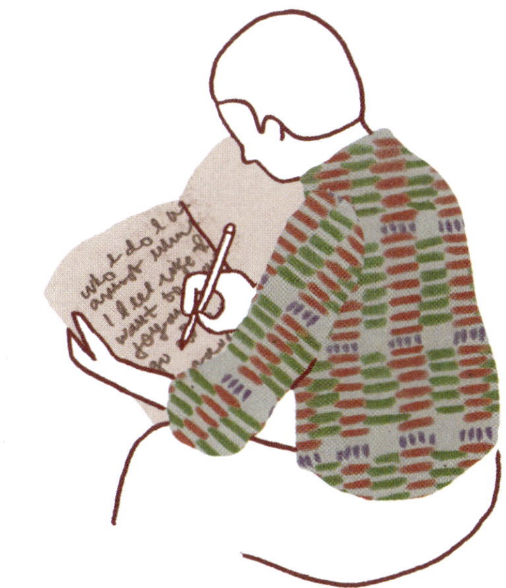

TRUST
THE
UNFOLDING

loosening our grip

Many of us live our lives under the illusion of control. We cling, white-knuckled, to the proverbial steering wheel, fearing what might happen if we loosen our grip. Not only is our vigilance exhausting but it rarely results in any change. Despite our attempts to control outcomes, much of the time, life unfolds as it will, and we either adjust to our circumstances or we resist them. Making peace with our limited control means we can relax into faith. If we believe that life is a great collaboration with something or someone beyond ourselves, then we can learn to trust the mysterious cocreators of our story—and enjoy the ride.

The next time you're feeling worried about a situation, ask yourself whether you have any power to affect the outcome. If yes, write down three concrete actions you can take, and then make an effort to follow through. If the situation remains out of your control, acknowledge that limitation and hand the outcome over to someone or something else—your guides, angels, ancestors, or God. Ask them to steer for a while. In other words: Do what you can, ask for help, and then let go. Trust that someone else, or the universe, will take care of it. As much as possible, dwell in this place of trust.

Stand on a bridge across a river or stream so that the water below flows away from you. As you watch the current, think about something in your life—a fear, a limiting belief, an attachment—that you want or need to release. Imagine sending it away with the rushing water, and say aloud, "I release ___." Take a moment, then go to the other side of the bridge and face the incoming current. Think of what or whom you want to summon into your life. Imagine inviting them with an open heart as the water streams toward you. Say aloud, "I welcome ___."

Close your eyes and imagine you are lying face down on the back of a giant animal—a bear or horse—your arms holding tight to her strong, soft neck as she lopes along. Give yourself over to the unpredictability of her movements. She is carrying you, and only she knows where she is headed. It is your job to hold on, adjusting your body according to her movements. You might offer her gentle direction, but you understand that her course is not up to you—and there is beauty in that. She may take you places you couldn't have dreamed of. Uncertainty affords possibility.

breakdowns and breakthroughs

The zigzagging Wildwood Trail in Portland, Oregon, is carved in hillsides dense with fern and trillium. Petite bridges hop over trickling creeks, jeweled by shafts of filtered light. I greet the massive fallen Douglas fir logs like old friends, noticing that, every time I pass through here, they seem to be feeding more and more new life in the form of moss, fungi, and even baby trees of varying species. As they decompose, these "nurse logs," as they're called, coddle their adopted young, providing nutrients, moisture, and protection. The forest contains innumerable layers, each generation of growth feeding off the last, illustrating one of nature's most elegant truths: When one being breaks down, it often means that another is breaking through. Although it can be difficult to appreciate in the moment, our own experiences of loss and dissolution often feed important new growth.

Childbirth offers a helpful analog. To be born, each of us must leave behind the safety and familiarity of the womb for the bright and bracing world beyond. In an instant, our whole universe collapses, yet at the same time, it radically expands. Similarly, when we experience what feels like a disastrous breakdown, we must remember that, with time and perspective, we may come to see it as life-giving—a breakthrough akin to taking our first breath.

In his eighties, my grandpa Henry said he'd finally achieved a bird's-eye view of his life. Looking back, he could see how the difficult chapters had contributed to the subsequent beautiful ones. As tough as it is to take this perspective while in the thick of our lives, we can practice zooming out to see the wider story.

Draw a spiral on a piece of paper. At the center of the spiral, write the word "BIRTH." In chronological order, working from the innermost rings toward the outermost, continue recording important life events along the spiral. Focus on moments of personal, emotional, or spiritual significance. While these might include events like graduation or marriage, feel free to think beyond traditional milestones. When you're finished, look back at the spiral and see if you can identify any particularly challenging times. What happened afterward? Did any gifts emerge? A deepening of relationship, a spiritual shift, or a new opportunity that wouldn't otherwise have arisen? Give yourself grace here; not every painful situation results in a breakthrough, and some take years and years to bear fruit. It's important to honor real suffering and give it time to unfold.

tether and weather

Imagine seaweed swirling in rough waters or a tall tree whose branches bow in a storm. Many plants subjected to harsh conditions survive by being flexible. Likewise, a cat that falls from a great height must relax its body to survive the impact. Many martial art forms, such as aikido and judo, teach the importance of yielding to what is coming our way—instead of blocking an opponent's punch directly, the practitioner allows it to pass over or alongside, letting the adversary's own momentum send them off course.

In a season of change, rigidity and tension cause brittleness; our resistance may break us. Acceptance of what is or has been, on the other hand, offers a pathway to peace and healing. This doesn't mean giving up; it means maintaining a state of openness, listening, and soft-bellied receptivity. In this state, we allow events to inform our understanding of the world, our direction, and how to respond. We're absorbing instead of repelling. Like trees in the wind, we let the world move us—and move through us.

While a tree's characteristics are largely determined by genetics (the thickness and pattern of its bark, the color and shape of its leaves, etc.), external conditions also shape it. We're much the same. From birth, we are shaped by our experiences. When subjected to a storm, we have a choice: We can grow tense, rigid, and brittle, or we can yield, rooting through the heart while letting the winds of change bend and strengthen us.

Sitting quietly, close your eyes and bring your awareness to your body. Beginning at the crown of your head and moving down to the tips of your toes, notice where you are holding tension. Does it feel as though you are bracing yourself against something? Is your jaw clenched? Your brow furrowed? Are your shoulders raised? As you move from head to toe, release the tension in each body part. Place your fingertips on your shoulders and roll them forward and back. Bring them to your brow and smooth the skin there several times. Place your tongue on the roof of your mouth and let your jaw go slack.

It's no wonder that children often wish to go barefoot, even in the cold. They are intuiting something we adults often forget or ignore—that for millennia, we evolved in direct contact with soil and sand, grass and stone. Our feet are powerful receptors, and reconnecting with Earth, or "grounding," has enormous healing potential. Studies have shown that walking barefoot or lying on the ground improves sleep, helps wounds heal more quickly, and alleviates pain and stress. Make a daily or weekly ritual of going barefoot outdoors. Slip off your shoes and socks and walk around in the backyard, at a park, or in a parkway strip. If you live near a beach, walk along wet sand. Even walking on wet pavement is effective for grounding.

a softening of hard edges

When I was around ten years old, my sister, my friend, and I took voice lessons together. We spent months preparing for our big performance, and when the time came, we were incredibly nervous. We bravely stepped onstage, circled the microphone, and began to sing. But we hadn't practiced with a microphone, and hearing our voices amplified throughout the auditorium immediately struck me as funny. I managed to hold back my laughter for a few beats, but when we hit a high note, I lost it. My uncontrollable giggles spread to my friend and sister, who erupted in laughter too. I remember looking out at the disapproving faces of the adults in the audience as the pianist ushered us off the stage. But there was one woman who had laughed along with us, and after the concert, she eased our shame by telling us that she had giggled all through her wedding vows. Our laughter wasn't a misfire but a natural response to tension—the body's wise way of releasing pressure.

As the middle child of five, my dad learned to use humor to diffuse household tension, and later he applied that skill as a father. When my sister and I were worried, he would often encourage us to say our fears aloud in a silly voice, which was a brilliant way to remind us not to take them too seriously. A puppeteer, playwright, and theater director, Pa's "characters" sometimes visited when one of us was in a sour mood. There was whiny Baby Gigi, who always outdid our complaining (and irritated our mom to no end); the clumsy giant Gumpus, who caused chaos by knocking things over; a hunchbacked witch who would burst out of the bathroom unexpectedly, a towel draped over her head like a shawl; and others. No matter how we were feeling, it was virtually impossible to keep from laughing when these visitors came around.

Laughter so elegantly softens the hard edges of the human experience. For many, it is a salvation—a lifeline at an impossibly difficult moment. Our capacity for humor is a sacred gift.

Ask yourself when you last enjoyed a good belly laugh. What, or who, brings you mirth? Plan to find your way to laughter soon. Or if laughter feels out of reach, start with a simple smile. Even when you don't feel like it—*especially* when you don't feel like it. It may seem counterintuitive, but making yourself smile can conjure something to smile about. Often, this small act is enough to shift your mood in the moment. Try smiling at a stranger in public and observe how they almost instinctively mirror you, returning the gesture. Notice the rush of satisfaction you feel over this shared connection.

Lightheartedness eases everything; it is medicine. Can you infuse tough moments with light by weaving humor into and around them? Try stepping outside yourself. Create a comedic alter ego, a character who helps you see your own troubles differently. Speak your worries in their voice, or think of the funny ways they might navigate the challenges you face.

We all have embarrassing stories. Trade yours with someone you trust. Laugh heartily with one another. When viewed from the right distance and through a humorous lens, even our most cringe-inducing memories can become medicine. Like shared tears, shared laughter reminds us that we're not alone. It can release us from the shame we've been carrying.

way will open

the path will find us

Which path is the right one? So often, we fret over which road to take. We focus on strategizing, on forecasting what will happen—so much so that the idea of listening for direction doesn't even occur to us.

Consider the migrating butterfly or bird, the salmon as it swims toward the ocean, or the wolf traveling hundreds of miles in search of a mate. As far as we can tell, each of these creatures is guided not by careful planning but by instinct. Their bodies know what their minds may not. We, too, have access to instinct and intuition, but our minds often ignore or override what our bodies tell us.

The Quakers have a saying—"way will open"—for when we are at a loss for what to do next. This phrase suggests that the answer we seek might not be reachable through analysis or calculation. Quakers traditionally sit in silence, waiting for the spirit to move or inspire them. If we simply get quiet and listen, the saying advises, the answer may reveal itself.

When the way forward feels impossible, impassable, like the turbulent sea crashing against rock, it's important to pause, remind ourselves of our truth, then wait and observe. The way will open. The tide will recede to reveal a smooth, sandy beach on which to walk. When the chosen path is aligned with the heart, signs of affirmation often appear. Obstacles that felt insurmountable may dissolve before us. If we commit to putting one foot in front of the other, looking neither too far ahead nor glancing behind, we can learn to trust that the path will find us.

"First thought, best thought." My sister relies on this maxim when faced with a tough decision. While she may not take action based on her first thought, listening for it provides her with valuable clues and prevents overthinking. But what if we can't recall which thought came first? One option is to flip a coin (yes, really!). Once you've seen the result, close your eyes and pay attention to any subtle signals your body gives you, especially the initial ones. How does this choice make your body feel? Do your shoulders tense up? Does a pit form in your stomach? Do you feel like you can't take a full breath, or are you breathing a little more deeply? Sometimes, when we force a decision to be made, our own instincts kick in, and we become aware of our true desire.

Go to a neighborhood you have never visited and walk a distance without an agenda or map for guidance. (Walking offers a nice, slow pace for this activity, but you can also ride your bike or drive a car.) Allow yourself to be guided by the environment. Follow what piques your interest, like the way a shaft of warm sunlight falls on one side of the street. Let go of the need to know where you're headed—or even where you are in each moment—and surrender, instead, to your inner compass. What do you notice? How does it feel to move through the world in this way?

When our conscious minds are confounded, we can explore guidance offered by the unconscious realm. One reliable way to access this wisdom is by noticing and interpreting our dreams. Similarly, we can keep an eye out for synchronicities—coincidental events that seem to be related in a meaningful way. If you aren't used to paying attention to synchronicities, it can seem as though they don't happen to you. Likewise, if you aren't in the habit of noticing your dreams, you might think you don't dream at all. But the more attention we devote to unconscious insight, the more often it tends to arise. It's as though, by paying attention, we raise the antenna, tuning to a new frequency.

Start by keeping a synchronicity and dream journal. If you're thinking about someone and they call you that same day, record the event in your journal. If you hear an interesting snippet of conversation at the post office, write it down. Before sleep each night, open your journal to a blank page and place it at your bedside along with a pen or pencil. The moment you wake, before your dream slips away, write it in your journal. Perhaps you recall the entire plot of your dream, or maybe it's just a detail or two—a phrase, an image, or even just a feeling. Revisit these notes regularly, especially when you're at an impasse or lacking direction. What signals have you been receiving lately? If you have a question or are facing a difficult decision, you can even try setting an intention to dream about it. As you're lying in bed, about to fall asleep, bring your attention to the question or topic you'd like to explore, and see what unfolds in the dreamworld.

plants take care of us

Last summer, the holy basil in my garden was prolific. The three plants I had seeded bushed out and claimed several feet of ground, their purple spires feeding all manner of pollinators. Like a pollinator myself, I returned to this patch again and again each day to give thanks and pluck a few leaves for a nourishing tea. I didn't research what holy basil was "good for," medicinally; I just felt it calling to me. Finally, out of curiosity, I looked up the plant's ancient medicinal uses. It didn't surprise me to learn that, for centuries, it had been used to treat the very symptoms I was experiencing at the time. Though I couldn't have told you why I felt drawn to the plant, I trusted in the mysterious attraction, and it led to healing. The earth provided in my time of need.

I keep hearing similar stories. Just the other day, a friend who is going through a period of deep depression said that Saint-John's-wort, a plant used to treat depression in herbal medicine, had popped up all over her yard. If we're paying attention, the right plants might make themselves available to us at just the right time. These plant allies have great gifts to share: There are those that soothe our anxiety, those that build up our resilience, those that offer to expand our vision, and those that will generously ease our pain. They may appear in the garden or yard spontaneously, or we may come across them in the wild. Perhaps we don't even encounter the physical plant but notice that its name keeps showing up, in books, podcasts, conversations. However these plants arrive, they do so as powerful caregivers, and we can accept them into our lives as medicine.

Adaptogens and nervines—plants that have been shown to support the body in times of anxiety and promote mental balance—may be a valuable part of your worry medicine cabinet. Ashwagandha, holy basil, skullcap, astragalus, and passionflower are all known to alleviate stress. For anxiety relief, seek out tinctures or teas containing these plants from a reputable herbalist.

If you're seeing a certain plant frequently or feeling particularly drawn to its color, shape, or smell, come into relationship with it by learning its name. This is an initial way of showing respect. Get curious about why you might be drawn to it, and listen for what the plant is asking you to do. (To observe it? To sit with it? To breathe in its scent?) If you feel drawn to harvest the plant, ask its permission first and listen for a sign of affirmation—a rustling of the leaves or the sudden chirp of a nearby bird. Offer something in return: Collect the plant's seeds to propagate it, sing to it, water it, or make some other gesture of reciprocity.

To take your relationship with this plant even further, explore its folklore. During the Victorian era, for example, flower varieties were steeped in symbolism. Chamomile meant "patience in adversity" and valerian meant "readiness." Even the color of a flower was loaded with meaning. Consider whether the plant's history or symbolism relates to what's going on in your life right now.

For at least five thousand years, humans around the globe have been drinking tea—infusions that soothe like a warm embrace. Make a ritual of preparing wild tea. Bring a thermos or camp stove with you to the garden or woodland and mindfully gather gifts from the earth. You may be surprised by what you can find in your own backyard; red clover, mint, pine needles, and violet are all common and make wonderful infusions. Before preparing your tea, be sure to research whether the plants you've encountered are safe to consume. (This information is abundant online, but Peterson Field Guides or Sam Thayer's books are excellent print resources.)

what if?

There are two kinds of worries: real-problem worries and hypothetical-problem worries. Like it sounds, a real-problem worry centers on what is actually happening, while a hypothetical-problem worry concerns what may be happening or what we fear will happen in the future. We think most of our worries are of the real-problem sort, but many, if not most, deal with hypothetical problems. When a worry pops up, ask yourself: “Do I know this to be true? How do I know it to be true? Could it be that it is not true?” Do you find that you’re asking lots of “what if” questions? If so, then it’s likely you’re catastrophizing. While hypothetical problems can certainly feel real and do have real effects on our minds and bodies, we shouldn’t fuel them with attention and mental resources. To keep them in check, we can start by calling them what they are—fear-based thoughts. From there, we can practice gently detaching ourselves from the thoughts, focusing, instead, on what is before us in the present.

We humans have powerful imaginations, easily picturing worst-case scenarios. But do we dare use our imaginative gifts to visualize the best, most beautiful scenario? Can we harness the power of "what if" to imagine and seek that which we most desire? A teacher of mine often says that when we wish for something to happen, we should "imagine it already so." When we visualize the ideal outcome in great detail, we plant the seed for it to become reality.

The "third eye" concept is present in many belief systems, such as Taoism, Hinduism, and Buddhism. Positioned on the brow, just above the space between the eyes, it is thought by many to be the seat of our intuition, inner vision, and imagination. Massaging this spot may invite clarity. With your hands in a prayer position, place your thumbs over your third eye and massage in a circular motion for two minutes. Notice how you feel afterward.

There is great power in writing things down. Sometimes, seeing our dream in writing helps us to visualize and even achieve it. Try writing the news headlines you wish to read. Maybe it's "Government Drastically Increases Funding for Schools, Healthcare" or "100 Species Deemed No Longer Endangered." Don't limit the headlines to what you might actually see in a news story. They can also be personal, such as: "Woman Impresses Panel During Job Interview, Assumes New Position" or "Couple Reunites After Three Years of Separation." Experiment with optimistic headlines to address a nagging concern, redirecting your imaginative powers in a positive direction.

Even though our worries are often conjecture, our bodies can't tell the difference between a real threat and an imagined one. To release your worry over a hypothetical problem, ground yourself in the present by looking into the mirror. Ask yourself whether you are safe in this moment. If yes, then gently reassure yourself, just as you would a child. Simply saying "I am safe" or "I am okay" aloud can be helpful. Next, think of an affirmation to remind yourself how resilient you are. For example, if you are worried about being or becoming ill, you could say, "My body is strong and wise." Or if you are worried about finances, you could say, "I trust in the abundance of the universe," or "I have everything I need." If you aren't sure what to say, try using this affirmation of release: "I release this worry. I am choosing not to fear." You can return to these affirmations again and again, as often as you need to.

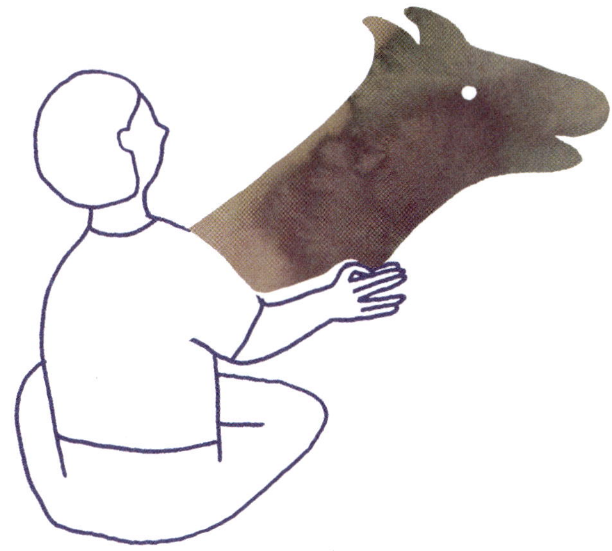

we are woven

together

creatures of the flock

How birds navigate the skies is still a mystery. Are they guided by the sun or more distant stars? Topography, memory, magnets? They navigate together, for thousands of miles, and they are stronger as a flock, flying in formation, than they are individually. There is so much wisdom in this unity of direction, this intuitive knowing, this togetherness.

We, too, are creatures of the flock. Throughout history, humans have lived in communities in which they not only cooked and ate together but danced and sang, worked and rested, celebrated and grieved together. Now, in modern times, we hardly know our neighbors. We may live in cities alongside hundreds of thousands of others and connect with vast numbers online, yet still so many of us feel deeply alone. We try to navigate our troubles and worries on our own, but anxiety breeds in isolation. We need to be seen, heard, and witnessed by others. Togetherness is a balm.

While the redwoods of the Pacific Coast are the tallest trees on Earth, their roots are surprisingly shallow. Instead of going deep, they go wide, interlocking with the roots from all the other trees around them. With the support of its neighbors, each individual redwood can withstand up to two thousand years of storms. Like these trees, we are designed to hold each other up, to be woven into community. Our hearts are healed as we braid ourselves together, feeling worthy, supported, and loved.

Crafting has long been a source of communal enjoyment. Get together with a friend or friends to do a craft. Collaborate on a project or work independently; both offer a sense of togetherness. Crafting circles are a bit like sitting around the campfire—the focus isn't on any one individual but on a nonhuman element, a source of warmth and generativity at the center of the group. Gathered around the literal or metaphorical hearth, self-consciousness can dissipate, and a lively, naturally evolving conversation will ensue. If crafting isn't appealing or accessible, try a game night or coworking morning with friends.

As much as possible, take care to surround yourself with others whose energy and attitude nourish you. Someone with a cheerful manner or hopeful orientation, for example, will invite you into that way of seeing. This may seem obvious, but it's not uncommon to fall into relationships with others who bring us down. We may seek these relationships in an unhealthy, maladaptive way, or we may have simply misjudged someone's character. To be clear, this doesn't mean that our friends and close companions should never challenge us. Of course they should! But ask yourself whether the points of challenge are good-natured and mutually fruitful. How do you feel when you come away from interactions with this person? Do you feel energized, even after a tough conversation? Or do you feel depleted? Are you fully yourself in the company of this person? The answers to these questions can tell you a lot about the health and fit of the relationship—which contributes hugely to your well-being.

Make a point to interact meaningfully with the people you encounter daily. Instead of asking "How are you?" when you greet your neighbor, try out, "How are you feeling today?" Or, if the conversation progresses, ask them what they've been learning about lately or what's been lighting them up. Connect more deeply with a coworker by asking her about herself. The next time you're standing in line or riding public transportation, put away your phone. Take out a sketchbook instead, or your latest knitting project. You may be surprised by the interactions this invites. Alternatively, simply make eye contact with someone and smile. Even little exchanges like these can contribute to our overall sense of belonging.

the jewels within

From the moment we are born, we receive countless unearned gifts. We didn't earn our parents' love or the water we drink. We didn't earn the beautiful sunset or our innate talents. The gifts I've been given that I didn't earn stand out in the pages of my life story. My friend Mobie brought me a homemade potpie when I was sick and single-parenting for a week. Without my asking, my friend Andrea lent me her car when mine broke down the day before a road trip. My sister, Sonya, brushed and braided my hair when I was completely overwhelmed two days after giving birth. These small but potent acts of kindness have shown me the sacred power of gift-giving. What a blessing to receive such tenderness and equally a blessing to offer it.

Each of us enters the world with a cache of jewels inside us. These jewels are our natural talents and abilities, the unique gifts we are meant to develop and offer to our community. The Dagara writer and spiritual teacher Malidoma Somé shares that "the healing

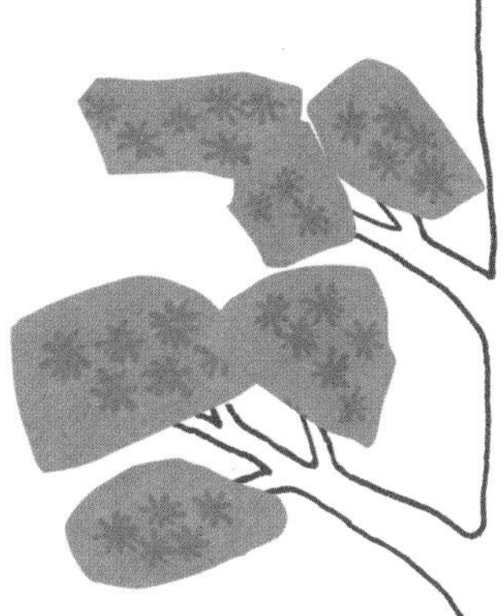

power of giving" is central to indigenous philosophy. According to Somé, the Dagara believe that illness stems from "the inability to deliver our gifts." By giving away the gems within us, we not only improve the lives of those we encounter but we find purpose and contentment.

The world is a beautiful, intimate web of reciprocity, and breathing perfectly demonstrates this. Each inhalation of oxygen we take is a generous gift from the trees around us, sustaining our existence. In return, our exhalations of carbon dioxide feed the trees' growth. Take a moment to stand or sit among the trees. Close your eyes and focus on the rims of your nostrils, where the outside air enters and the inside air exits. Visualize a thread connecting your breath to the trees around you. Each breath is not only your own but shared. Feel the harmonious exchange of inhale and exhale. Can you sense the depth of nourishment available to you? Notice, too, the sustenance you offer in return.

◎

When we serve others, we shift the focus away from ourselves, and our own anxieties are eased. Look for daily opportunities to be of service. You might simply move an insect out of harm's way, call a friend who is lonely, or buy lunch for a person in need. Try engaging in some form of service every day for a week and observe how your own anxiety shifts.

◎

Each of us has a gift to offer, whether it's a warm meal, a reassuring embrace, or a listening ear. We also possess the grace and humility to receive—to be comforted and held. Our most fulfilling relationships involve a balance of both. Propose an exchange of worries with someone dear to you. This could take the form of a written correspondence, a call, or an in-person meeting. As your dear one expresses what's on their mind, simply listen (or read) with compassion. In your response, try not to judge or counsel them. Avoid referring to yourself. Simply validate and honor their experience by reflecting it back to them with phrases like, "What I'm hearing you say is . . ." When they've said all they wish to say, trade roles. Share vulnerably, and let the other's deep listening comfort you. If both parties consent, the exchange might open into a conversation in which each of you offers or requests guidance. Other times, the mutual sharing might be enough to create a positive shift for one or both of you.

the seed that needs fire

Fire is an agent of change, and it plays a necessary role in many ecosystems. For example, pyrophytic plants need fire to reproduce. Redwood and lodgepole pinecones require the extreme heat of fire to melt the thick resin coating their seeds. Once "unlocked," the seeds can germinate, allowing the next generation of trees to surge forth. Likewise, Baker's wild hollyhock, a lavender-colored goddess that blankets the ground after a wildfire, has seeds that can lie dormant for over one hundred years until another fire comes to catalyze them.

We, too, may need an intense, heated moment—perhaps even a crisis—to spur our growth. A devastating breakup, the loss of a job, or even a life-threatening illness can prompt necessary change or realignment.

For years, a friend of mine was unhappy and underappreciated at her job but was too afraid to quit. Then, one day, her boss unexpectedly let her go. While, at first, my friend was disoriented and angry, this crisis ultimately set her on a path toward founding her own organization—a dream she'd held for many years. She thrived in her new role and was able to offer her gifts to the community in a way she could not have done previously. She burst brilliantly from the ashes, a fuller and more vibrant version of herself.

Fire is dangerous, but it can also be a friend, creating the conditions for new life. Emergencies contain aspects of emergence. That is, everything that happens to us can contribute to some form of future growth. Let us trust that the crises in our lives, though deeply challenging, will "unlock" our potential to flourish.

On a small piece of paper, write down something you're worried about—or write an idea or habit you wish to release, something that is no longer serving you. Make a fire in a fireplace or firepit and feed your paper to the flames. Watch it slowly curl inward, blacken, and disappear. If possible, cook over your fire, transforming your worry into nourishment.

Each morning, before you switch on any artificial light, make a ritual of lighting a candle. This can be an especially powerful practice in the depths of winter, when the days are short and many of us wake to a dark sky. Like the blackest soil, the predawn darkness is incredibly fertile. Speak aloud to the flame your intentions, the seeds you wish to plant. Tell it what you would like to see germinate—today or in your life in general.

peace invites connection

Riding the subway after a stressful day at work, my friend Gloria noticed a commotion. People were shifting around, pointing. The crowd parted to reveal a delicate orange butterfly fluttering around the train car, bumping into windows and trying to find a way out. Like a gentle breeze, the creature's presence immediately softened Gloria's mood. She felt herself relax, the tension melting from her body. Without meaning to, Gloria started speaking to the butterfly in her mind. "Don't worry," she thought, "we'll stop soon and you can fly away." Almost immediately, the butterfly landed on her pant leg, where it stayed until the train reached its next stop. Gloria stepped onto the platform, the butterfly clinging to her leg as she walked through the tunnel and up the steps. As she emerged into the daylight, the creature took flight, disappearing into the open air.

Always, always, we are giving off energy—and the energy we emit is the energy we invite. When we're stressed, we're more likely to complain, be impatient, and snap at our loved ones. Our energy may repel those around us without our realizing, or we may be so consumed by our worry that we miss extraordinary moments containing the medicine we need. When we cultivate peace within ourselves, we transmit the same to our environment. The world around us senses our peace, and often it returns the gift. People and animals may be drawn to us, recognizing that we are safe and comforting company. (My daughters and I call this a Snow White state of mind.) Our awareness, which had been narrowly focused on our own distress, can expand to include the beauty that surrounds us—a great source of spiritual nourishment. By inviting calm, even for a few minutes a day, we become more receptive to the healing states of connectedness and awe.

Visit a place you feel drawn to in your backyard, at a local park, beach, or riverbank, or in a nearby forest, and simply sit quietly. Assume any posture you find comfortable, on the ground or in a seat. Remain in stillness for at least twenty minutes. Begin to observe your surroundings and watch as they shift. Does the wind pick up or die down? Do the clouds transform, casting new shadows? What do you notice around you, and what do you notice within you? How would you describe the energy of your thoughts and feelings? If your thoughts are racing, your energy frantic, can you invite them to settle? As you sit, you might be visited by an insect or a bird. You might be inspired to ask a question—silently or aloud—to the trees, plants, and other beings around you. Listen closely for a response. The world is sentient, alive. It craves our loving attention, and it wants to help.

On a different day, in another season, return to the same spot and notice its dynamism. How does it—and how do you—feel different?

Animals are our allies. In many religions and cultures, certain animals are considered sacred spiritual guides. Pay close attention to the animals you encounter, and notice when a particular creature crosses your path repeatedly. If you saw the animal in the wild or in a piece of art, what were you doing or thinking about when you encountered it? If the animal appeared in your dream, what moods or sensations accompanied it? Consider what qualities you associate with the creature, or if you wish, look up the traditional meanings it may represent. The animals might have a message for you about a situation in your life. See if you can decipher what it is.

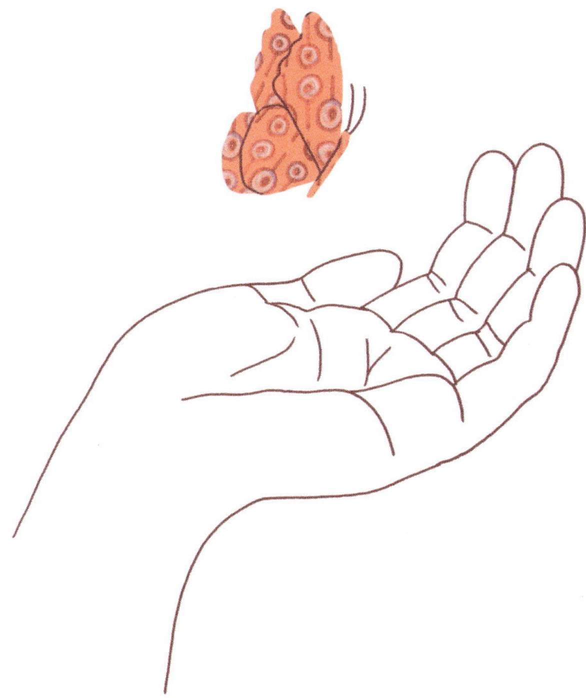

play

upside down at the bank

At four, my daughter was doing headstands—dozens each day. I often wondered if it was healthy to do so many. Her urge to flip upside down was so strong that every wall in our house soon bore her footprints. She stood on her head at Lee Street Beach when we were visiting my parents, her hair grinding into the sand, uncaring, as we adults shook our heads, thinking of the arduous bath time ahead. And I'll never forget the headstand she launched into at the bank, legs propped against the teller's desk. During that era, every adult who visited our house was challenged to a headstand, and those who accepted often surprised themselves, delighting in their body's beautiful ability to remember. Even my dad, seventy-year-old Grandpa Mike, made an elegant inversion, gingerly landing his feet between picture frames on the living room wall.

How often do we play as adults? As we move out of adolescence, we're taught to de-prioritize play as our world begins to revolve around productivity and accomplishment. From an early age, we're asked, "What do you want to be when you grow up?" as in, "What will your job be? How will you make a living?" and not, "What will make your heart vibrate with joy? What will excite you and give you life?" Instead of standing on our heads, we adults live in our heads, often ignoring our physical and spiritual needs.

Play is a powerful tool for soothing anxiety because, simply put, enjoying ourselves melts worry away. While a friend nervously awaited the results of a medical scan, she and I spent an especially playful weekend together. We didn't set out to prioritize play, but we found ourselves swimming, playing music, and laughing with abandon. This was powerful medicine for her anxiety and a reminder that healing can be playful and play can be incredibly healing.

My neighbor recently rediscovered her childhood love of roller-skating. Now she goes to the rink weekly, sometimes several nights in a row, taking classes, sailing around to energetic tunes, and feeling the wind in her hair. In the same spirit, I went to the waterpark with my daughters this past summer and relived a glorious part of my youth, shooting down the slides countless times. Can you revisit the playfulness of your youth or find the adult equivalent of what you enjoyed as a child? Commit to indulging the playful part of your spirit, which is in all of us. Give yourself permission to do something just because it's fun and feels good—bake brownies, go sledding, or challenge your partner to a board game. To give these activities the importance they deserve, schedule them just as you would a meeting or appointment.

What would it look like to invite a spirit of play into your daily life? Approach something routine in a fresh, experimental way: Go grocery shopping with your headphones on, bobbing your head to music as you make your way down the aisles (maybe even busting a move!). Take an unfamiliar route to work, singing in your car as you go. Even switching up your typical hairstyle or trying a new cuisine can add lightness and color to your everyday.

chasing chickens

When one of our hens flies the coop, I delight in watching my daughter try to catch her. Just as she closes in, the hen evades her grasp, eliciting shrieks of frustration. Recently, watching this familiar scene unfold, it occurred to me that my daughter's frantic chase is not unlike my nightly efforts to fall asleep, my mind darting this way and that while I struggle to tame it, growing more and more agitated with each failed attempt. When my daughter finally catches her hen, they both look satisfied. I watch the creature surrender in her arms, even closing her eyes as my daughter strokes the feathers on her back. This is our task at night: to still the frenzied mind, soothing it with a compassionate caress.

When I can't fall asleep, I often think back to the sleepless nights during my childhood. "Just close your eyes and rest," my mom would reassure me. "Rest is just about as good as sleep." By focusing on the benefits of simply quieting the mind and body, we can take some of the pressure off the slumber itself. So I take deep breaths, my exhales longer than my inhales, and I open my eyes wide, letting them close slowly and heavily several times in a row. Sometimes, I'll count backward from one hundred, nodding off before I'm halfway to zero.

But there are still those untamed-chicken nights—the hours of fitful pursuit when my mind is racing, my exhausted body chasing it. I commit to tabling my worries till tomorrow. "My only job is to breathe in and breathe out," I think. Slowly, and then all at once, the worry dissipates, and I let myself be held.

Call to mind a place where you felt complete joy or comfort. In as much detail as you can, visualize returning to it. What do you hear and smell there? How does being there make your body feel? For me, this place is my grandparents' house as it looked during my childhood. If I can't fall asleep, I often return to that house in my mind, turning into the driveway, walking on the paving stones, noticing the bushes in front of the picture window, and hearing the dog bark. I feel the cold brass doorknob in my hand and, as I enter, sense the golden light streaming through the door's stained-glass window. Room by room, I walk through the house in my mind, eventually drifting off to sleep.

Lie on your back on the floor near a wall and swing your legs up so they rest vertically against it, your feet facing the ceiling. You can place a pillow under your lower back for extra support. This yoga pose, known as Viparita Karani, or Legs Up the Wall, is often recommended to alleviate middle-of-the-night anxiety and stress. You can stay in this pose for up to fifteen or twenty minutes, depending on your comfort level. Viparita Karani activates the parasympathetic nervous system, also known as the "rest and restore" system, allowing the body to relax and heal.

If you can't sleep, step outside for some deep, delicious drinks of the night air, or simply open your window and lean out for a similar effect. Notice the quality of the night—the breeze, the temperature, the sky, the shadows. Let the sounds of the night be a lullaby. Your bed may feel even cozier when you return to it.

what will be watered
by our tears?

like the purifying rain

Sometimes we need permission, space, and time to fully feel—an invitation to sit with our anxiety, cry, purge, and cry some more. Crying is the body's ancient and intelligent way of releasing the pent-up tension, grief, and hardship that comes with being human. Not only does crying release stress-relieving oxytocin and endorphins, but tears contain leucine enkephalin, a natural painkiller. Tears are salty, like drops of ocean water, reminding us that we are made of the same elements as Earth and the cosmos. Like the purifying rain, tears stream down our cheeks, cleansing our wounds before nourishing the earth.

In modern Western culture, tears are somewhat taboo. While babies and children cry easily, adults are expected to contain their sorrow, expressing it outwardly only in private or with a close confidant. Western funerals typically involve gathering with others, but only those closest to the deceased are expected to weep, and the grieving family often asks for privacy following the service. But throughout most of human history and across the world, grief has been communal. In some traditions, it is believed that one's sorrow or pain shouldn't be kept private. Grievers are encouraged to cry openly, and others will join them. Grief rituals involving collective wailing—or "keening" in Celtic culture—can act as a pressure valve for the whole community. Embedded in these rituals is the understanding that challenging emotions are meant to gather and discharge regularly, like clouds delivering a brief rain shower before moving on. When we suppress our difficult emotions, they only grow stronger, threatening to erupt like a storm with the power to overtake us. Can we allow our tears to fall, giving ourselves over to this natural and age-old form of release?

Strike one stringed instrument near another, and the second instrument will sound the same note. This is called acoustic resonance. Similarly, we experience emotional resonance with one another; often, when we see someone else cry, tears well up in our own eyes. This shared expression offers us a chance to release our own emotions as well. Watch for opportunities to support a friend navigating difficult emotions. Offer the great gift of your undivided attention. It may move something within you too.

Sometimes we feel numb or blocked, and we need help finding sweet release. Listening to a moving song can bring us to tears and help us let go of tension. A poem, novel, film, or other artwork may stir us in the same way. Make time to experience your emotions fully and hold yourself very gently as they move through you. Ask yourself: What will be watered by my tears?

One of my favorite parenting tips is to "just add water." When my daughters are bored, agitated, or buzzing with pent-up energy, I know it's time to start the bath, fill up the kiddie pool, or play in the sink. For adults, too, interacting with water can be incredibly soothing and restorative. If you have access to a river, lake, or ocean, find your way to the water's edge and sit. (If you can't access a natural water source, prepare a nourishing bath.) If the moment feels right and it is safe to do so, immerse yourself in the water. Think of something you want to shed, and let the water wash it away. If tears begin to flow, let them merge with the infinite drops that surround you. How does it feel to be held in the arms of this ancient friend?

a reflection
of
the
sacred

creativity in crisis

In periods of tumult, creativity can transform worry. During a devastating infertility journey, a friend wrote a moving book of poetry. Frida Kahlo famously painted throughout a lifetime of physical pain, and the Romani people in Spain endured hundreds of years of persecution, during which they developed flamenco—a soulful dance that is now a defining aspect of Spanish culture.

Both individually and collectively, we humans have always metabolized hardship through creation. Yet, from a young age, many of us are taught that creativity is a special skill, that some people are inherently "creative" while others are not. This view not only prevents many of us from accessing the powerful medicine inherent in creating but also misconstrues the nature of creativity altogether. Creativity is a reflection of the sacred in every one of us, an expression of our vital force and a line of connection to the holy. It is our birthright. And each of us can tap into its mysterious healing power at any moment.

I don't consider myself a poet, but in times of uncertainty, I've taken to writing and reading poetry. There is something about the looseness of the form and the immediacy and universality of its emotion that make it a brilliant companion in hardship. Two poems I turn to again and again are "The Conditional" by Ada Limón and "For Calling the Spirit Back from Wandering the Earth in Its Human Feet" by Joy Harjo—but poetry is incredibly personal, and you may wish to sample many voices before you find one that speaks to you. Ask around among friends for poetry recommendations. Borrow a book of poetry, if you can, or seek one out at your local bookstore or library. (Staff recommendations or book reviews can offer helpful tips.) If you're particularly moved by a poem, try memorizing it. When we commit something to memory, it becomes a part of us, and we can call it to mind in difficult moments.

Try your hand at writing a poem. There are countless ways to do this, but if you aren't sure where to begin, simply list the emotions you've been feeling lately. Perhaps you're frustrated, relieved, confused, or hopeful. (It's very likely you're experiencing many feelings at once, and not all of them consistent with one another.) Next, look around you, and record what strikes or interests you about your physical environment. Be as specific as possible and pay careful attention to sensory information: What do you see, feel, smell, taste, or touch? Finally, try weaving these two worlds together on the page: the inner and the outer, the emotional and the sensory. Remember that you don't have to produce anything polished to share. This is simply a way for you to express your unique experience.

Many adults are intimidated by drawing, feeling pressured to produce something "good." Yet, somehow, very young children fearlessly put pencil to paper. Tap back into this childlike spirit by drawing with your nondominant hand. When we do this, we're less likely to expect a perfect result, so we are freed from judging it too harshly and can embrace the fluidity of our creation. Alternatively, take a long look at an object, landscape, or person and try drawing the subject with your eyes closed. Let go of any need to control the outcome of the drawing. You are employing the creative force that lies within each of us, collaborating with the Mystery. Allow yourself to be surprised by what you create without "trying."

Movement can also be creative, and there is great medicine to be found in letting your body move intuitively. To lift your spirits, put on some music you love and dance freely. Do this solo or with friends and family. If you find you're overthinking your movements or feeling self-conscious, try drawing the curtains and turning out the lights. Sway, rock, let your body lead the way. To discharge worry, shake like a dog emerging from water or try letting out a sound as you move. (A wail? A howl? A roar?)

STILL
THERE
IS
MUSIC

bathing in song

a group in my community regularly holds "song baths," during which they gather around someone in need of healing and sing to them in soothing, harmonic voices. Our bodies, composed mostly of water, resonate with sound waves, creating a profound internal stirring when we are surrounded by music. As we bathe in song, the sound waves permeate our tissues, and the result can be transcendent. Music has the power to give us chills, make us weep, and put us in touch with the divine.

Each of us is born making music. From six weeks in utero, our hearts begin to beat a rhythm we carry with us our whole lives. Incredibly, the heart rates of choral singers have been shown to synchronize during communal singing. Not only does singing reduce stress but it releases oxytocin, the hormone of love and bonding. When we sing together, we experience deep connectedness—we become one. This might explain why singing and chanting have been integral to so many cultures and religions throughout history.

In her book *Dancing in the Streets*, Barbara Ehrenreich suggests that the decline of traditional rituals and festivities in the early modern era, which often included communal singing, contributed significantly to a rise in melancholy and depression that persists to this day. We are hardwired for song—each of us has a voice, yet how many of us sing regularly? How many of us play music not just to improve our skills but for the sheer joy of it? How often do we let sound soothe, move, and heal us?

In our darkest hours, music remains. Still, there is music.

When I'm feeling anxious or down, I often hum softly to myself. There is an inherent leisure to humming that signals to the body that everything is okay. (Consider the word "humdrum," which means "ordinary" or "uneventful"). Humming also stimulates the vagus nerve, which is connected to the vocal cords and plays an important role in the parasympathetic nervous system, easing our body's stress response. The next time you're worried or agitated, try humming. You may feel your body relax and your mood lift.

Make it a daily or weekly habit to sing or play music, either by yourself or with others. Some of us might feel shy about singing in public, but in a group, voices have a wonderful way of merging—there are no "good" or "bad" voices, just the beauty of imperfect unison. If possible, find a friend or a group to sing with. In my own community, a folk school hosts a monthly song circle; perhaps there's something similar near you. If not, consider starting one! Many folk choruses and informal singing groups use a call-and-response method, in which a leader "calls" and the other singers "respond," imitating her. Even if you don't know how to read music, you can join one of these groups and learn to sing in harmony.

Bells are central features of temples and churches worldwide, in part because of their divine ability to purify and soothe. Certain sound frequencies are believed to reduce anxiety and promote healing. Listen to live bells, singing bowls, or even bees buzzing. Notice how you feel when you tune into this music. Where do your thoughts travel, and what are your dreams like afterward?

everyday
alchemy

it's all compost, baby

Every evening, our family's big compost bowl overflows with bread crusts and apple cores, the remnants of meals and snacks enjoyed throughout the day. The other night, on heaving the weighty slop into the pile outside, the words of an old mentor sprang to mind. "It's all compost, baby."

As every gardener knows, manure makes the best fertilizer. The hard rinds, the discarded parts, the dirty peels, the moldy bits—all become vital nourishment. Waste feeds fecundity. Decay cultivates life. Each of us has the alchemical power to transform the "shit" that happens to us into fuel for our growth, helping us build capacities we will need in the future.

What if we considered everything a source of nourishment? Can we learn to compost the aspects of ourselves we don't like? What about our mistakes? Can we throw all our experiences into the compost heap and let them fortify us?

Like the cells in our bodies, we are constantly rebuilding and renewing ourselves. We can change gradually, shifting our habits over time, or we can make a sudden change, quitting a job or ending a relationship that no longer serves us. Every moment offers a new opportunity to align ourselves more closely with who we are or who we want to become. Consider reaching out to an elder you know and interviewing them. Ask them to share one regret they have and one revelation that changed the course of their life. If you aren't in contact with an elder, search for interviews with elders on YouTube. Their reflections on life can offer valuable perspectives on transformation and growth.

Self-compassion is essential to composting the past. When you find yourself worrying about a past action, try simply saying, "I honor who I was in the past and hold space for who I'm becoming." Our mistakes, properly metabolized, enrich the soil in which we grow.

My friend Ike started having seizures when he was barely twenty years old. In and out of medical settings constantly over the years, in his thirties he founded an organization that sends handmade cards to hospitalized children. According to Ike, we can use what happens to us as "insulation or inspiration." Our challenges can harden us, forming a protective barrier around our hearts, or they can prompt the creation of something beautiful. While not every negative experience can or should inspire us, we are never without this alchemical power. What stories do you tell to protect yourself? Ask yourself whether this "insulation" is serving you. Might it become inspiration instead?

tending

Years ago, my partner and I rented a little farmhouse on fifty acres. Decades before we arrived, someone had planted a hundred blueberry bushes and several fruit trees on the land. They bore a luscious harvest, which we enjoyed and shared with our neighbors. To pay forward the gift, my partner added more and more trees to the orchard, knowing they wouldn't mature until we'd gone. Since then, we've moved several times, planting fruit trees wherever we go in a spirit of gratitude.

A fruit tree is love embodied, and its gifts are twofold: The tree itself offers its fruit, which is in turn the gift of a grower's toil. When we harvest from a fruit tree, we experience the earth's love for us and also the love of another human, often a stranger, who cared enough to tend to something for our benefit.

The act of "tending" is powerful medicine, especially for anxiety rooted in disconnection. I once knew a woman who collected wilted houseplants from trash cans and curbsides, brought them home, and revived them. But tending can be as simple as feeding the birds in winter. It can look like creating a "watering hole" for bees in the summer by placing a shallow dish filled with water and stones on your porch. It can even be passive: In the fall, instead of raking the leaves in your yard, let them rest on the earth, offering food, shelter, and nesting material to countless creatures. These are acts of care in service to the natural world; acts that say, *I am a vital member of my ecosystem*; acts that stitch us into place, affirming our belonging.

Grow something from seed. Even a lentil or an avocado pit is likely to sprout when planted. Many of us cherish childhood memories of the outdoors—the loamy smell of soil or the tickle of an earthworm in our palm—but we seldom relish in these sensory joys as adults. Immerse your hands in the soil, tend to the plant babies that emerge, and savor the gifts they offer in exchange for your care.

What fruit trees or berry bushes grow well in your area? Identify a few options, and ask your neighbors which they would most enjoy. Plant a tree or bush in your own yard that will bear that fruit. By involving your neighbors, you share your bounty even before it arrives. Simply considering others, asking for their input, is a profound act of care. When your tree or bush bears fruit, invite your community to harvest it with you. Deliver whole fruit or a pie to a friend. Even if you move away, your orchard or berry patch will continue to provide for the community—in fact, it will go on providing for generations to come.

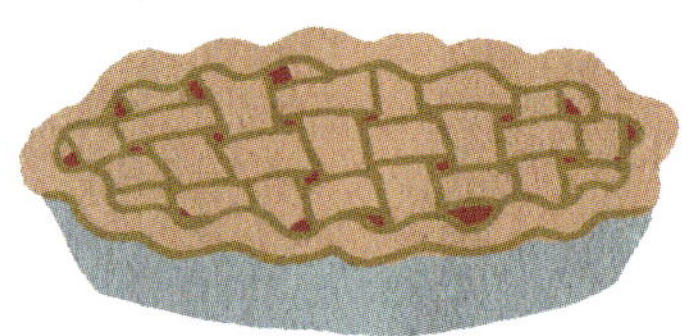

remaking the world

In our troubled world, there is no shortage of heartbreak. Endless wars wage on, racial and economic injustices continue to unfold, and the earth suffers the consequences of human shortsightedness and greed. But a broken heart is also a heart cracked open, offering us a chance to expand beyond our usual notions of self. While it's natural to self-medicate or seek distraction in the face of pain, we should not turn away from our sorrow, nor should we pathologize it. Instead, we can consider it a guiding light, illuminating what needs our energy and attention. This pain is a gift, helping us uncover our limitless compassion and love.

The world runs on stories. Concepts of "us and them" and "good and bad"—these are stories we've agreed to tell and retell in the form of our institutions: systems of capitalism, mass incarceration, border enforcement, and more. But we humans wrote the stories, and that means we have the power to revise them. The beautiful truth is that there is meaning and purpose in remaking our world for the better.

Taking action involves us in the stories we tell. Though acting is often more work than merely witnessing, it can relieve us of our anxiety, which thrives on stagnation.

The sheer number of crises calling for our attention can feel overwhelming. We cannot hold the whole world on our shoulders—and we don't have to. Remember that the small strands each of us pulls affect the integrity of the whole fabric. Across the globe, someone else is also tugging, helping to unravel legacies of harm.

Our task is to get quiet so we can sense what is truly ours to do. Where are we most needed? What are we called to offer? The world is remade with each sunrise. What a gift to be part of its unfolding story.

Make a strand of "worry flags," similar to Buddhist "prayer flags." Use paper or fabric for your rectangular flags, sewing or hot-gluing them along a piece of string. On each flag, use paint or markers to write or draw a meaningful word, phrase, or image that represents something you're worried about. For example, if you're preoccupied by thoughts of war, you could write "liberation for all beings" or draw a dove of peace. If you're worried about the climate, you could write the names of some of your favorite natural places. Hang the flags outside, if possible, on a porch or balcony or along a fence. In the Tibetan Buddhist tradition, it is believed that as the wind rustles the flags, they release our prayers for the benefit of all. The flags will likely fade as they are weathered by the elements, reflecting the natural passing of all things. Consider burning your flags once they've frayed or fallen apart, releasing the last of your worries in a cleansing fire.

We often build walls to shield ourselves from pain, fortifying our defenses. But what if we saw ourselves as vessels for transformative change? The Tibetan Buddhist practice of *tonglen,* meaning "giving and taking," is an active prayer for the dissolution of suffering: Sit quietly and open yourself to the world's pain, taking it in on one deep inhale. Hold your breath for a few counts at the top, visualizing a powerful alchemy within as you transform that pain into healing. As you exhale slowly, release loving compassion. Send it to yourself, to the people you know who need it, and to those beyond your community. Repeat this cycle as many times as you wish. With each inhale, imagine a wave of the world's anger and sadness surging forth, lapping at the shore. Then in the softest, gentlest way possible, release it all, along with your wishes for universal healing.

acknowledgments

To my parents, who are never first to hang up the phone when we talk. Thank you for always encouraging my creativity. Thank you for your joie de vivre, which is like an ever-bubbling spring we all drink from.

To Nolan, I'm grateful for the wise perspective you continually offer me, for your steadiness in storms, and for our shared commitment to an unruly life together. Thank you for taking the compost out, by which I mean holding our whole household together during the creation of this book.

To my sister, Sonya, for the robust and ongoing exploratory conversations about healing this past year; it's my great joy and privilege to learn and grow alongside you. You keep the flames of inspiration lit, and I am so blessed to have you as sister and collaborator.

To my daughters, Lucia and Rio, you astound me every day with your depth of feeling and love, with your vivacious spirits. Thank you for all you are teaching me. And thank you for our afternoons drawing together.

Thank you to those who generously shared their medicine stories with me for this book: Gloria, Daniel, Monique, Sonya, Mom, Pa, Laura, Andrea, Mobie, Claire, Alison, Brandi, Kerri, Eric, John, Vince, and Samantha, among others. Many thanks to Ike Nwankwo for speaking with me about founding Cardz For Kidz, and to Reed Anderson, whose work inspired a practice in the "Hand We Wish to Hold" chapter.

A big thank-you to dear friends Corrinne and Dara, for cheering me on as I endeavored to write this book and for always being one voice memo away when I had an ounce of doubt. To Sonya, Nolan, and Corrinne for your crucial feedback early on. Thank you to Nicole Civita for helping me see myself clearly. Thanks to those dear ones who held space and made it possible for me to work on this book: my in-laws Laura and Doug and the wonderful Nancy and Scott at the Illustration Institute.

Enormous gratitude to my editor, Melissa Rhodes Zahorsky, for recognizing my vision from the start and offering invaluable editorial counsel. Thank you to Diane Marsh for the beautiful layout of this book, and thank you to the entire team at Andrews McMeel for the work in producing it. Thank you to my literary agent, Kate Woodrow, for your unwavering belief in me and for being such a solid guide and teammate.

To all my teachers, human and nonhuman alike, whose wisdom permeates this book: Stone, Water, Fire, Mother Earth, and our animal kin whom I apprenticed with over the last year. To Monique, who so skillfully illuminates the deep networks of support beyond the human realm, thank you for continuing to share the medicine our world so urgently needs. To writers Robin Wall Kimmerer, Malidoma Somé, Sobonfu Somé, Joy Harjo, Ada Limón, Ilya Kaminsky, Thich

Nhat Hanh, Martín Prechtel, Caitlin Doughty, Charles Eisenstein, and Martin Shaw, for pollinating my heart and mind with your profound teachings.

Thank you to my ancestors, who, as dedicated artists, writers, and musicians, passed down the everlasting truth that creative expression fills life with meaning.

I extend gratitude to the land I reside on for holding me and providing for me and my loved ones—and to the Miami, Delaware, Potawatomi, and Shawnee people who have stewarded it for centuries.

Not least, I offer deep gratitude to the trees who became the paper for this book. And to all the people behind the scenes: those who worked hard to print it, and the postal workers, drivers, administrators, booksellers, and librarians who have given precious life energy toward putting it in readers' hands. I hope this book is worthy of these great efforts and gifts.

about the author

Nina Montenegro is a writer and visual artist whose work reawakens reverence, bringing to life the possibility of healing. With her sister, Sonya, Nina is the cofounder and codirector of The Far Woods creative studio. Her previous books include *Mending Life: A Handbook for Repairing Clothes and Hearts* and *A Year in the Garden.*

Enjoy *Worry Medicine* as an audiobook, wherever audiobooks are sold.

Worry Medicine: Remedies and Rituals for Anxious Times

The authorised representative in the EEA is Simon and Schuster Netherlands BV, Herculesplein 96 3584 AA Utrecht, Netherlands. (info@simonandschuster.nl)

Amber Lotus
an imprint of Andrews McMeel Publishing
a division of Andrews McMeel Universal
1130 Walnut Street, Kansas City, MissourI 64106

www.andrewsmcmeel.com

25 26 27 28 29 IGV 10 9 8 7 6 5 4 3 2 1

ISBN: 978-1-5248-9765-9

Library of Congress Control Number: 2025934751

Editor: Melissa R. Zahorsky
Art Director: Diane Marsh
Production Editor: Elizabeth A. Garcia
Production Manager: Julie Skalla

The information and practices offered in this book are for educational purposes only and should not replace professional medical advice, counseling, or therapy. Seek guidance from qualified professionals for personalized support.